FULL DISCLOSURE: GETTING TO REAL MARKET VALUE

Cap Gemini Ernst & Young presents *Invisible Advantage* to selected clients and friends. We believe it offers a unique perspective on how intangible assets—those items that don't typically show up on a balance sheet or income statement—drive economic performance. Since the Center for Business Innovation's groundbreaking study "Measures That Matter" discovered that institutional investors base one-third of their portfolio allocation decisions on intangibles like brand and innovation, we have been intrigued with the concept of intangible management, measurement, and disclosure.

Through a series of case studies and best practices in intangible measurement, the authors outline the twelve most important "invisible" value drivers: leadership, strategy execution, communication & transparency, brand equity, reputation, alliances & networks, technology & processes, human capital, culture, innovation, intellectual capital, and adaptability. They also outline a strategy for managing these intangibles—and as the authors point out—those who take the lead, will *set* the standards.

To learn more about this topic, or to find out how you can participate in our *Invisible Advantage* Forums and Seminars, please contact Jon Low at 617-761-4032 or jon.low@us.cgeyc.com, or visit our website at www.InvisibleAdvantage.com.

INVISIBLE ADVANTAGE

How Intangibles Are Driving
Business Performance

Jonathan Low and
Pam Cohen Kalafut

PERSEUS
PUBLISHING

Copyright © 2002 by Cap Gemini Ernst & Young, U.S. LLC
Library of Congress Control Number: 2002102645
ISBN 0-7382-0539-7

Perseus Publishing is a member of the Perseus Books Group.
Find us on the World Wide Web at http://www.perseuspublishing.com
Perseus Publishing books are available at special discounts for bulk purchases in the United States by corporations, institutions, and other organizations. For more information, please contact the Special Markets Department at the Perseus Books Group, 11 Cambridge Center, Cambridge, MA 02142, or call (800) 255-1514 or (617)252-5298, or e-mail j.mccrary@perseusbooks.com.

Text design by Janice Tapia
Set in 11-point Berkeley Book

First printing, April 2002

1 2 3 4 5 6 7 8 9 10—04 03 02

To our families

CONTENTS

ACKNOWLEDGMENTS

This book could not have been written without the guidance and assistance of many people. It was a truly the collaborative effort of a wide network. First and foremost, we wish to thank Chris Meyer, the Director of the CGEY Center for Business Innovation, who provided unstinting support, encouragement, and good counsel. Our team at the CBI—Audrey Boldt, Jonathan Robinson, Mukul Kanabar, Prabal Chakrabarti, Alice Wang, and, particularly, our lead research assistant, Eric Chen, were simply invaluable.

Sarah Mavrinac, now at INSEAD Business School, has been a constant source of gifted research advice and enjoyable collaboration. Our former colleague Tony Siesfeld was "present at the creation." Much of our success is due in no small measure to his contributions.

CGEY colleagues from the United States, Canada, France, Italy, the United Kingdom, Norway, Denmark, Poland, Switzerland, Australia, and New Zealand provided inspiration and assistance. Larry Rothman, Roberto Panzarani, Michael Schulz, Andre-Benoit de Jaegere, Calvin Cobb, Paul Bierbusse, Richard Seurat, Michael Krenek, and Chris Christensen have been particularly steadfast. Our former colleagues at Ernst & Young LLP also urged us on and proved helpful allies. Teddy Wivel's efforts are especially worthy of note.

We owe a great debt of gratitude to other members of the community of interest that has evolved around the growing importance of intangibles. Former SEC commissioner Steve Wallman, now CEO of Folio Trade, and Margaret Blair of Georgetown University Law Center were inspiring and stimulating leaders of the Brookings Institution's

Task Force on Intangibles to which we were pleased to be able to contribute. They provided early encouragement for the idea that this book should be written. Greg Wurzburg and Graham Vickery of the Organization for Economic Cooperation and Development (OECD) have been valued friends and wise counselors on the policy implications of these issues. Larry Prusak heartened us by his own example. He also proffered much-needed skepticism about overreliance on numbers as ends in themselves. Professor Claes Fornell of the University of Michigan, Professor Baruch Lev of New York University's Stern School, Professors David Larcker and Chris Ittner of The Wharton School, and a host of equally talented researchers such as Ulf Johanson, Leandro Canibano, Paloma Sanchez, Mary McCain, and Laurie Bassi have, over the years, been generous with their time and have stimulated us with their ideas.

Mike Malone and Geoff Baum of *Forbes ASAP* magazine shared our enthusiasm for this subject. They provided welcome support for our research efforts as well cosponsorship for a pair of conferences that led to the writing of the book. Peter Moore, the founder of the Snowmass Forum, furnished wisdom, encouragement, and friendship. Leslie Gaines-Ross of Burson-Marsteller, Colonel Tom Tyrrell of the U.S. Marine Corps, and Barry Bates of Compaq contributed insights, ideas, and their most valuable asset—their time—to help us.

Before we embarked on this enterprise, we were warned by colleagues that writing a book was the third most painful, nonlethal civilian experience after building a house and having a baby. Nick Philipson, Dave Goehring, Elizabeth Carduff, and their colleagues at Perseus Publishing proved them wrong. They have been the soul of courtesy and collaboration. It has been a pleasure working with them. Our agent, Rafe Sagalyn, has always been there for us with sound instruction and incisive guidance.

We gratefully acknowledge the debt we owe to John Case. He is wise, unflappable, and inspired. He was a joy to work with. We have tried to figure out how to say it without sounding trite, but the truth is, we couldn't have done this book without him.

Finally, heartfelt thanks to our families: Tim, Noah, Dave, Murphy, and Island Dog in the Cohen Kalafut family; Kathleen, Travis, Nathaniel, and Libby in the Low/Kroll household. Your unwavering support in the face of mood swings, missed meals, and frantic preoccupation can not be repaid in any tangible way.

PART ONE

The Intangibles
Economy

INVISIBLE ADVANTAGE

Peek behind the scenes of a business success story and you're likely to find what we call an invisible advantage. It's an advantage that the company in question understands and utilizes, but one that competitors can't easily copy. For example:

- Everybody knows about McDonald's famed franchise system—one store sold at a time, no regional territories— and its rigorous quality-control procedures, which ensure that McDonald's products and services will be nearly identical from one store to another in any given country. But how many people know about what one wag dubbed the "real estate sandwich"? In the early days, the McDonald's parent company was short on cash and deep in debt; it couldn't afford to grow. Financial maven Harry Sonneborn, a partner of McDonald's CEO Ray Kroc, hit on the idea of buying up store sites (or leasing them on a long-term basis), then charging rent to franchisees. This rent would be either a minimum rate—still plenty to cover the costs plus a markup—or a percentage of sales, whichever was larger. Over the years, sales and prices rose, McDonald's real-estate costs remained constant, and thanks to the company's innovative strategy, the money rolled in.[1] The profits that fueled McDonald's growth into a global powerhouse didn't come from hamburgers but from an intangible—the efficient execution of a strategy based on real estate.

- In 1994, two scientists working at Pfizer were administering trial studies of the drug Sildenafil as a new heart medicine when they discovered that it also increased blood flow to the penis. The rest is history: Sildenafil became Viagra, approved by the U.S. Food and Drug Administration on March 27, 1998, as the first pill to treat erectile disfunction. It was an instant blockbuster, exactly the kind of drug that has fed the ever-growing market valuation of big pharmaceutical companies; in 2000, for example, it generated $1.34 billion in revenues (not to mention garnering the company millions of dollars' worth of free publicity). Incredibly, however, Viagra is *only one of eight* drugs in Pfizer's product line that brought in more than $1 billion in revenue that year. It wasn't even the largest: That honor went to Lipitor, a cholesterol medicine, which generated more than $5 billion.[2] What seems at first glance like a lucky accident—the discovery of Viagra—is in fact a product of a global-scale research-and-development effort that operates largely out of the public view.
- Thirty years ago, Pratt & Whitney products—notably its JT8D engine—accounted for 90 percent of the commercial aircraft jet-engine market. General Electric (GE) then began to catch up to Pratt and eventually surpassed it. One key was GE's newer technology. A second advantage was GE Capital. Thanks to GE's creative organizational structure, the company's aircraft-engine unit had a built-in source of financing that companies relying on outside financing couldn't beat.[3] Following the same model, sales of GE Medical Systems' big-ticket equipment are often financed by GE Healthcare Financial Services (GE HFS). When executives of a five-location mammography center were contemplating buying the latest GE radiography equipment, the chief financial officer knew that no bank

would be willing to finance the deal on the terms the center required. GE HFS provided the center with a low monthly payment, a twenty-four-month cancellation option, and an early-buyout option—exactly what the chief financial officer (CFO) wanted. GE recognizes that the organizational and social value inherent in reducing its cost of capital and that of its customers is a crucial advantage. That value can be passed along to enhance the already high quality of the company's products, leading to higher sales and deeper customer relationships.[4]

- The luxury brands owned by the $40-billion French company LVMH Moet-Hennessey Louis Vuitton S.A. have plenty of cachet; these include not only those in the company's name but also Christian Dior, Dom Perignon champagne, the Sephora cosmetics chain, and many others. But a well-known name doesn't necessarily translate into a profitable business (think of Rolls-Royce automobiles). Behind the scenes, the management team assembled by chief executive Bernard Arnault has created a flurry of activity.[5] New LVMH designers—many of them not French—have roiled the fashion industry, winning the company that elusive quality "buzz." The company began focusing on selling through its own retail shops rather than through licensees, improving its control over the image of its brands.[6] It also began paying close attention to manufacturing costs, thereby boosting profit margins. "Off the runways," said one report on the company, "LVMH behaves like a cost-conscious maker of discount goods."[7] LVMH assembled a portfolio of intangibles—in its case, brands. It uses other intangibles, such as its marketing clout, to cross-sell these luxury items while employing its organizational skills to reduce costs and increase internal efficiencies.

The list of examples could go on, because in today's economy advantage, time and again, accrues not to the company with the biggest factories or the deepest pockets but to the company that does the best job of managing its intangibles.

Intangibles refers to many different aspects of a business. It's the strategy that Kroc's partner, Sonneborn, came up with—and it's McDonald's ability to execute it, quickly and quietly, before competitors or anybody else caught on to what they were doing. It's the highly specialized knowledge that GE Capital brings to a financing deal, knowledge about how to tailor a deal to suit a customer while still making money on the financing transaction. It's the R&D investment of a Pfizer, the careful brand management of a LVMH.

And it's much more besides. People. Ideas. Know-how. Relationships. Systems. Work processes. All they have in common is that they drive economic performance. They don't show up on a balance sheet or an income statement—yet, they are the manageable and usually quantifiable drivers of corporate-value creation. They're the source of invisible advantage.

❀　❀　❀

Our proposition is, quite simply, that intangibles are already transforming the way in which you run your business, manage associates, design your products, sell your services, and interact with your customers. And that transformation will continue. The implications are profound for your strategy, for balancing your long- and short-term decision-making, for your corporate reputation, for communications and disclosure, and for the government policies that shape the world around you. The sources of value creation are changing. How you manage will change as well. You are probably already aware of these trends. You may even be attempting to assess their importance to your organization. Our objective is to provide a framework for how to consider this metamorphosis and offer some ideas on what to do about it.

Phrases like *brand equity*, *intellectual property*, and *human capital*—all references to certain kinds of intangibles—have become part of the business lexicon. Companies trumpet their ability to innovate or their commitment to quality. They call their employees "associates," and their leaders announce that "people are our most important assets." Even so, we're not sure that businesspeople have truly understood the opportunities offered by a focus on intangibles—or the threats that arise from neglecting them.

Do you know, for example, how much of your company's valuation is attributable to intangibles? Research (which we'll describe in detail in chapter three) shows that *fully 35 percent of portfolio managers' decisions about where to allocate their investment dollars is based on intangibles.* Incredibly, these are facets of the business that most companies don't measure, manage, or disclose. Wall Street analysts and sophisticated investors use them anyway to gauge a company's strength and prospects. How much more value could a company create by focusing on the intangibles that are central to its business—and letting Wall Street know exactly what it was doing and why it was doing so?

Are you aware of the many kinds of intangibles that *customers* are suddenly demanding? Consumers want information about food's nutritional content, and about the conditions under which it was produced ("dolphin-free" tuna, nongenetically modified corn, for example). They want to know what a company is doing to protect or preserve the natural environment—and whether or not any of its products or production processes degrade the environment. They ask if products are manufactured in factories with poor labor conditions. In business-to-business markets, customers demand to know about intangibles, such as whether a supplier is ISO-qualified or not (International Organization for Standardization), what its defect rates are, and if it has a good safety record. The media that cover your company, the prospective employees who may be deciding to join you, even the nongovernmental organizations that evaluate your business from the standpoint of their own social or environmental agenda—all are customers for information about the intangibles that affect them. If differentiation is a key to success, here are grounds for differentiation—of precisely the kind that customers have shown they care about.

Have you watched what happens when companies *don't* pay attention to intangibles? In the months following the 1999 allegations of "tainted" Coke in Belgium, the Coca-Cola Company lost $34 billion in market value; profits of the company's European subsidiary fell by $205 million;[8] Coke's proposed acquisition of European soft-drink giant Orangina was rejected by the European Commission;[9] and the CEO lost his job soon after.[10] All this stemmed from an episode in which the facts were in dispute. The market reaction, however, was so severe because the damage was to intangibles: The company's reputation for unimpeachable leadership, for sterling brand management, for effective communications, and for sensitivity to the nuances of alliance and network management. The failure (or perception of failure) across so many crucial indices was acute. But you don't need a reputation-shattering disaster to be hurt by poor management of intangibles. Just look at all the companies that have suffered from faulty brand stewardship, sluggish innovation, or contentious labor relations. Poor management of intangibles can hurt a company quickly, as in the Coca-Cola case, or slowly, as in the gradual decline of Polaroid, which a generation ago was the leader in family photography and on October 12, 2001, filed for reorganization under Chapter 11 of the U.S. Bankruptcy Code.

THE VALUE OF INTANGIBLES

These threats and opportunities arise because intangibles have *value*. Value lies in the skill and knowledge of the people who manage a business and those who work for it. It's incorporated in the relationships and reputations a company establishes—with suppliers, with customers, with partners and stakeholders of all sorts. It's built into how a company operates: the ideas that it pursues, the innovations it can bring to market, the information systems that tell managers what is going on in the world and in the organization. Businesses may have been slow to think systematically about intangibles, but they can hardly help acting on, and reacting to, the value that markets of all sorts have begun to place on intangibles. Consider just a few examples.

People

How much is one individual worth? When Texas Rangers shortstop Alex Rodriguez—"A-Rod," as he is known to sports fans—became a free agent at the end of the 2000 season, people in the know expected him to land a record-setting contract. But when the Texas Rangers agreed to pay him $252 million over ten years, they were assigning A-Rod a value that was $2 million *greater* than the amount the club's owner had paid just two years earlier for the entire team, its stadium, its minor-league affiliates, and its spring-training facility.[11] Crazy? Only if the popular shortstop doesn't help win enough games and bring in enough fans to earn his keep. In the business world, look at IBM's 1995 acquisition of Lotus Development Corporation. Big Blue spent $3.5 billion not only to get Lotus's valuable Notes program but also, many people suspected, to get the services of a single programmer named Ray Ozzie, Notes's creator. (After the acquisition, Ozzie's colleagues began calling him the "three-billion-dollar man."[12]) When Lotus CEO Jim Manzi resigned ninety-nine days after the deal's closing, there was speculation that Ozzie and his colleagues might leave too, taking most of the $3.5 billion in assets—their brains—with them. But Ozzie stayed on for another two years to help make Notes, with IBM's assistance, as successful as possible.[13] Lotus Notes today is used by 60 million people.

But it isn't just the odd superstar who carries value in today's economy. When large companies acquire smaller ones—IBM's more recent acquisition of a tiny e-strategy consulting firm called Mainspring is just one example—as often as not what they're buying is the small firm's people. Internally, companies have begun paying unprecedented attention to the recruitment and retention of employees. Recruitment is now no longer a human-resources function; at many companies, virtually every senior manager plays a role. Retention is tracked carefully; managers' job evaluations sometimes depend on their ability to retain key people. Concern with retention can spill over into many other areas of a company. When our predecessor firm Ernst & Young learned that its female partners were leaving at a rapid rate, for example, the company mounted a major initiative to discover why—and to make the changes that would encourage women to stay, such as setting up an Office of Retention focused on retaining women employees.[14]

Of course, the combination of high salaries and unusual perks that flourished during the dot-com era was partly a reflection of tight-as-a-drum labor markets. What's instructive, however, is how companies acted during the subsequent downturn. Those that had hired new college graduates and then found that they had to rescind their job offers didn't simply cut the graduates adrift, as they might have in the past. Instead they encouraged the young people to defer their employment for a year, and often paid them bonuses of up to three months' pay. Our consulting firm, Cap Gemini Ernst & Young, forced by the recent economic slowdown to cut costs, offered some professional employees the chance to take furloughs, rather than just be laid off, enabling employees to take home a percentage of their salary, plus benefits, while working fewer hours. This practice has allowed CGEY to reduce costs while still maintaining a working relationship with people on whom the firm has already made major recruiting and training investments. And, of course, as the economy begins to pick up again, these employees will return to full-time, not only reducing the necessary amount of new recruiting and training, but also greatly shortening the firm's lag time in capitalizing on new business opportunities.[15] Other companies, such as Cisco Systems, offered some laid-off employees the chance to spend a year at a nonprofit, with Cisco paying a portion of their salaries, their benefits, and any stock-option awards they were eligible for. More than 200 Cisco employees expressed interest.[16]

Information Systems

It's tempting to think of an information system as a tangible asset because it utilizes computers. Don't make that mistake. The hardware is definitely tangible. But the particular configuration of software and data—and the business uses to which the information is put—are not. And it's through those configurations that companies can create huge amounts of value.

Take the familiar story of Dell Computer. Everybody knows about Dell's vaunted build-to-order system, by which buyers order customized PCs over the phone or the Web. Dell has established systems that allow it to build a PC in a day or two and have it in the customer's hands in another day or two. On the financial side, as has often been noted, Dell gets its customers' money before it pays for parts and labor and thus is always operating in a positive cash-flow situation.

But this capability—itself an astonishing example of invisible advantage—turns out to be only part of the story. Unlike its competitors, most of which manufacture in batches and sell through dealers, Dell is in direct contact with end-use customers and thus gets market information well before competitors do. That allows it to constantly adjust its pricing to market conditions, much the way airlines constantly adjust the price of seats on a flight. Revised market forecasts are shared with suppliers every week, and Dell doesn't hesitate to lean on those same suppliers for immediate price reductions when conditions warrant. Sales managers know at any given instant exactly what it costs Dell to manufacture a given PC and are free to adjust retail prices on the spot.

Talk about the value of an intangible! When PC sales slowed in early 2001, Dell promptly cut its prices so sharply that its net margin slipped nearly two percentage points. In doing so, however, it gained market share—and it was the only one of the top six PC manufacturers to turn a profit in the first quarter of the year. Competitors Hewlett-Packard and Compaq Computer, by contrast, had to take big writedowns in that quarter for unsold inventory.[17]

Relationships with Customers

"Customer relationships" is a category that encompasses brand management, customer service, and many other facets of a business's operation, all of them interrelated. Some of the buzz-phrases of the past decade—customer intimacy, one-to-one marketing, the lifetime value of the customer—testify to the growing realization in the business world of its importance. One of the factors that sustains Amazon.com's market value, for instance—still at $4.5 billion in mid-2001 even after falling 85 percent from its peak—is the widespread view that Amazon has established remarkably close and positive relationships with a huge base of customers. Online shoppers are greeted by name. Gentle suggestions are offered about books or other products they might be interested in. Compared to many other e-commerce sites, Amazon's online purchase process is easy and pleasant, its after-purchase service superb, the information gathered about customer preferences rich and deep. If the company never made a dime, all these tools and techniques for keeping close to customers would still be worth plenty to a potential acquirer.

A recurrent theme throughout this book is that no intangible is an island, complete unto itself; rather, astute management of one intangible depends on astute management of many others. So it is with customer relationships. Amazon's intimacy with its customers, for instance, depends on an information system that is itself a source of enormous value. Or, for example, take Singapore International

Airlines, which is legendary among travelers to the Far East for its commitment to customer service. Its brand icon—the "SIA Girl," used in every advertisement—is widely recognized, and is a kind of personification of the airline's commitment to service. Employees learn that they are responsible for maintaining a high level of service. The airline spends 15 percent of its payroll on employee training, in contrast to 1.5 percent by U.S. airlines. Flight attendants get four months of training, compared to an average four weeks in the United States.[18] A quarterly "service-performance index" is closely watched throughout the airline as a benchmark for internal evaluation.

SIA's management of a crisis—the kind of test that Coca-Cola flunked—protected its customer-friendly reputation rather than destroying it. In October 2000, SIA experienced its first deadly crash in twenty-eight years: An accident in Taiwan killed 81 of the 179 passengers aboard. The next day, the airline offered $25,000 to families of those who died to help cover immediate expenses. When it was determined that the crash was due to pilot error, SIA immediately offered each family an additional $400,000, five times what it was required to pay in liability cases. Cheong Choong Kong, deputy chairman and chief executive, said the airline accepted "full responsibility" for the crash. No other airline in the world has ever moved so fast, been so generous, and accepted its responsibility in quite this manner.[19] SIA was acting to protect what it perceived to be its most valuable assets: the intangibles of brand, reputation, and leadership based on treatment of its customers.

This is just a sampling—a foretaste—of the value of intangibles, and of how they can affect a company's performance. In the chapters to come we'll examine many more categories of intangibles, and we'll look at many more examples of effective and ineffective management of them. Our purpose is partly to give you dozens of fresh ideas about how to do things differently in your business so as to *build*, *retain*, and *increase* the value that resides in intangibles.

But we have a more general goal as well, which is why we devote the next two chapters to a little history and research. We want to begin changing the way businesspeople all over the world think about the assets they are charged with managing. We want to provide a new perspective—a new focus—that is required in today's economy. Once you *really* understand intangibles, you'll never run a company the same way again. You'll operate by new rules. You'll create and learn to track new performance measures—measures that look forward as well as backward, that show how you're likely to be doing in a year or two as well as how you did last quarter. (Too many businesspeople today still run their company by looking squarely into the rearview mirror.) You'll keep your eye on aspects of your business that can't easily be counted, but that are essential to the company's future health. You'll see your operations through some of the same lenses that many of your most sophisticated investors—not to mention customers, lenders, and current and potential employees—are already using to evaluate your company, which means you'll be better able to manage the variables that they're watching and assessing.

The intangibles we focus on in this book are certainly not the only ones. Others of greater importance may emerge in the future. But these are the ones that both our clients and our research have identified as the most important now. There are twelve: *leadership, strategy, communications, brand, reputation, alliances and networks, technology, human capital, workplace/culture, innovation, intellectual capital,* and *adaptability*. It's around these drivers of value that we will build our story.

The story of intangibles—of how important they have come to be in today's economy, and how companies can begin to manage them the way they should be managed—is a story, we think, that badly needs to be told. It is the subject of this book.

THE RISE OF THE
"INTANGIBLES ECONOMY"

A century ago, the world was undergoing a series of economic trans-
formations every bit as dramatic as those taking place today. In the
United States, for example, the railroads and telegraph had opened up
a national marketplace. Entrepreneurs such as Cyrus McCormick
(farm machinery) and Edward Clark (Singer Sewing Machines) were
building factories on a scale seldom seen in the past, and were turning
out manufactured products in unheard-of quantities.[1] Retailers such
as Marshall Field and John Wanamaker created giant emporiums for
shopping, while new catalog merchants such as Sears, Roebuck &
Company enabled rural residents to share in the outpouring of mass-
produced goods. The American Telephone & Telegraph Corporation,
led by Theodore Vail, began wiring the nation for instant voice communication, elbowing competitors aside or buying them out. The
Standard Oil Company under John D. Rockefeller at one point owned
virtually all of the petroleum business. It was an age of size. What
mattered most in the marketplace, so it seemed, were big factories, big
distribution networks, deep financial pockets, operations on a grand
scale.

Look just a little below the surface, however, and the picture becomes both more complex and more interesting. Take the most important industry of the new age, automobiles, and its iconic leaders,
Henry Ford and Alfred P. Sloan. Ford and Sloan, too, would operate
on a large scale. But what ultimately distinguished first one and then

the other from the competition was an eye for the invisible advantage—for creating value based on intangibles.

When Ford first set up shop in 1903, the world's auto industry was a bustling, fiercely competitive business.[2] But every manufacturer had one thing in common: They all practiced what is known as craft production. Skilled workmen cut and shaped individual parts and assembled them in place, honing and filing as necessary to make them fit. Very few shops anywhere in the world could produce more than 1,000 cars a year using this system, and each car was necessarily expensive. Ford's fundamental innovation, developed over the five-year period from 1903 to 1908 (as he created car designs ranging from the original Model A to the Model T), was to use interchangeable parts designed for easy attachment. That by itself allowed him to replace skilled fitters with unskilled laborers, and thereby to manufacture cars faster and cheaper than anybody else. But the crowning achievement of this system was the introduction, in 1913, of the moving assembly line—in Ford's case, metal strips attached to two parallel belts that ran the length of the factory.[3] With the assembly line in place, the time required for assembly of major components into a complete car fell from 750 minutes—twelve and a half hours—to 93 minutes, or about an hour and a half, an 88-percent reduction. The car that had cost $850 in 1908 cost only $290 in 1915.[4]

The mass-production system, as Ford called it, transformed the workplace. It's a particularly powerful example of the role of intangibles because it illustrates how two such factors, process improvement and organizational design, contributed to the work organization we still see today. (And its "grandchild," supply-chain management, is arguably the most important process improvement of our own time.) But mass production exacerbated a problem every manufacturing company of those days experienced to one degree or another: turnover in the workforce. The industrial jobs of the day were difficult and dangerous. The people who took them were often fresh off the farm or the boat, and were unaccustomed to factory labor. The assembly line made things worse; no longer could workers proceed at their own pace. So they quit, in large numbers, and often abruptly. Some 1,300 to 1,400 men at Ford's Highland Park plant were found "missing from their stations" every day. The factory had to hire 54,000 men in one year to maintain a workforce of 13,000, a turnover rate of more than 400 percent.[5] To combat turnover, Ford in 1914 adopted what might now be called a human-capital strategy. He announced that employees would henceforth work only eight hours per day, which was unheard of at the time. What's more, they would be paid an astronomical $5 for those eight hours of work. Right away, turnover plunged; not long after, it was as low as 37 percent. But sales and production shot up. Between 1914 and 1916 the company's profits rose from $30 million to $60 million.[6]

By 1920 Ford Motor Company was America's biggest auto manufacturer. Intangibles such as those mentioned above—strategy execution, adaptability, workplace/culture, technology, and human capital—had been important to its growth, but now its dominance was reflected in assets that were very much tangible. Ford owned huge integrated factories such as the 160-acre Rouge complex, all of them equipped with expensive machinery. It owned suppliers of raw materials and component parts. Of course, up-and-coming competitors such as General Motors, created in 1908 and in 1923 headed by an MIT graduate named Alfred P. Sloan, could and did build big, modern factories as well, and they could as easily buy up suppliers.[7] What eventually gave GM its own invisible advantage—and allowed the company to surpass Ford as the industry's number-one manufacturer—were some different intangible assets, ones that Ford had largely ignored.

One of Sloan's secrets was the creation of a portfolio of brands. Unlike Ford, who focused on offering a good-quality, affordable car ("any color the customer wants so long as it's black"), Sloan offered buyers a range of styles and prices. The brands were structured so that GM could move its customers to more expensive cars as their incomes and their families grew. Sloan also created a divisional organization, in which both car and component-part businesses were overseen by relatively autonomous general managers. The system solved the managerial problems that had been plaguing companies such as Ford. The new mass-production companies were simply too big to be run by a single chain of command. Headquarters couldn't know what was going on at the plant level. Plant managers couldn't respond to threats and opportunities without instructions from the corporate level. GM's divisional structure—essentially, the structure of the modern corporation—allowed the company to share costs over its entire operation while maintaining a high degree of flexibility at the operating level. It also enabled GM to reorganize quickly as market conditions might dictate. (Believe it or not, even GM was once nimble and innovative.) It gave the company an invisible advantage that Ford was slow to adopt.

Similar stories could be told about other industries; indeed, from one perspective much of the past century's business history can be viewed as the history of intangibles. Coca-Cola and Procter & Gamble, among many others, learned the techniques of creating and cultivating a set of emotions (including that all-important emotion called "customer loyalty") attached to a brand name. AT&T—followed quickly by the pharmaceutical industry—learned the advantage provided by an organized, well-funded research-and-development center. IBM in its heyday developed unparalleled technical skills in the design and construction of its computers, and unparalleled sales expertise in getting them into the hands of customers. 3M Corporation created a system of expectations and incentives that encouraged technical personnel to work on new products, thereby producing a stream of innovations.

And yet for most of the century, the discovery and management of intangibles was at best a haphazard affair, rarely an explicit part of corporate strategy. The management theorist Peter Drucker codified what Sloan had done only in 1946, for example—and only after reading Drucker's book *The Concept of the Corporation* did Henry Ford II decide to model the company he had inherited on General Motors. Meanwhile, remarkably few companies developed their capacity for innovation by copying AT&T's Bell Labs or the incentive system of 3M, and still fewer paid attention to intangibles such as corporate reputation or the ability to develop and execute strategy. Companies chose their leaders largely from within, rather than looking outside for the best available. Those leaders communicated with the outside world as little as possible. The job of the manager, taught in business school and on the job, was to manage the triad of financial indicators—sales, expenses, and assets—and very little else.

There was a reason for this, of course: The economy in the industrialized world of those days was structured differently. Many industries in the United States were tightly regulated by the government, while many in Europe were controlled by government-owned enterprises. In every country, plenty of markets were dominated by a few large companies. (America's Big Three—GM, Ford, and Chrysler—owned 95 percent of the domestic auto market in 1955.)[8] Competition in most free-enterprise economies was subdued, almost gentlemanly. Competitive advantage came mainly from brute size, through economies of scale, and from deep pockets. Moreover, the economy wasn't changing rapidly, so companies could do business one year pretty much the way they had done business the previous year. Technological evolution was led—and largely controlled—by companies already in a position of dominance. Upstarts were rarely able to challenge market leaders.

THE TRANSITION TO TODAY'S ECONOMY

And then came the change. Or rather the changes. Just to catalog them is to get an idea of how dramatically the economic environment has been altered in the last twenty or twenty-five years.

Services

Before anybody was talking about a knowledge or information economy they were talking about a *service* economy. In the United States, more than three-quarters of private-sector employees (and nearly all of those in the public sector) now work in some kind of service enterprise.[9] The figures are comparable in other industrialized nations. A belated sign of the times: In 1995, *Fortune* magazine finally included service businesses such as Wal-Mart Stores and Citigroup on an equal footing with manufacturers in its famous list of the 500 largest companies in America. (For some years before they had been relegated to a secondary and distinctly less prestigious list of their own.)

Service businesses are by definition different from manufacturing companies. Though they need facilities—offices, shops, computers, and so on—they don't require as much in the way of tangible assets as a manufacturer. They rarely need as much capital to get started. Many service businesses—health care, legal services, computer programming, financial services, business consulting—depend heavily on the labor of highly trained professionals. Much of their value, in the sense of their ability to deliver what their customers want, resides in the heads of these people.

New Technology

Everybody knows the stories about the invention and spread of computers—mainframes, minis, ultimately the personal computer itself. Nearly everybody has heard of Moore's Law; one way of formulating it is to say that the cost of a given amount of computing power falls by half every eighteen months. The Internet has spread more rapidly than any other form of communication—and it still has a long way to go. (Not many homes even in the United States are wired for any form of broadband data access.) Indeed, what's interesting about the computer revolution in general is that, for all the talk about "Internet speed" and the like, it has played itself out over decades. It will likely continue for decades to come.

Where business is concerned, the computer revolution had some effects that were not widely noticed. In the past, points out Leonard I. Nakamura of the Federal Reserve Bank of Philadelphia, one source of a large corporation's market power was its white-collar staff and sales force. Anybody might come up with new production technology, but no upstart could easily duplicate the costly sales and administrative infrastructure of existing market leaders. The spread of decentralized computing power, however, enabled (and encouraged) corporations to cut their sales and white-collar payrolls substantially. They promptly proceeded to do so: Beginning around 1980, sales and clerical staff began to decline as a proportion of the overall workforce. Trouble was, that left big companies vulnerable to competition from new entrants in their industry. An upstart might not be able to replicate an extensive network of people, but it could certainly replicate an extensive network of computers.[10]

Deregulation and Privatization

It's hard to remember now, but for most of the twentieth century U.S. airlines operated under tight regulations, their fares and routes (and even the price of drinks!) set by a government agency. The situation was similar in trucking and railroads. The financial services industry—commercial banks and brokerage houses in particular—was governed by strict rules. Telecommunications was the province of one large corporation, itself tightly regulated.

Today all that has changed. In the United States, electric power is only the latest in a series of industries to undergo deregulation. In other countries, deregulation has been accompanied by privatization—of transportation and communications utilities, of state-owned banks and oil companies, of government-run coal mines and factories. Market-oriented principles and policies prevail nearly everywhere. The day of the protected, regulated, government-sponsored or government-run enterprise is very nearly over.

Globalization

In 1970, U.S. imports and exports were each the equivalent of about 6 percent of the United States's gross domestic product. In 2000 the figure was 14.6 percent imports and 10.8 percent exports according to a U.S Department of Commerce Bureau of Economic Analysis.[11] So it was all over the world. The volume of world trade (in real terms) increased 435 percent over the last thirty years.[12] Americans found themselves buying not only Japanese-made cars and Chinese-made garments but Finnish cell phones and German business software. The growth in trade was accompanied by another trend, itself a distinctive aspect of globalization: a marked increase in both direct and indirect international investment. Japanese manufacturers now produce 60 percent of the cars they sell in the United States in American factories.[13] The German manufacturer Siemens operates 650 facilities (including 110 manufacturing and assembly plants) in North America. U.S. direct investment in other countries grew 54 percent just between 1994 and 1999. Meanwhile, companies have begun acquiring businesses and brands almost without regard to nationality. Ford owns Volvo and Jaguar. Many of the leading U.S. book and magazine publishers are owned by giant companies based in Germany (Bertelsmann), the United Kingdom (Pearson, News Corp.), or France (Hachette Filipacchi).

One corollary of globalization is that consumers and business buyers no longer have the bias they once had toward their own nation's products and services. McDonald's hamburgers, Mercedes automobiles, and Microsoft software are popular all over the world. Italian clothing, Japanese cars, and German machine tools are often thought to be superior to other nations' home-grown products. A second corollary: Companies are judged and evaluated by dozens of different standards. Europeans care more (so far) than Americans about genetic modification of food. African governments hold oil companies accountable for their effect on the environment. An Asian factory that provides relatively high-paying jobs for people coming out of rural villages may look like a sweatshop to Western eyes.

Entrepreneurship

The growth in the number of small companies—and the relative ease with which they can be started—is also an international phenomenon, but it's most pronounced in the United States. In 1990 there were slightly more than 5 million companies with employees in America. By the end of the decade the number had risen about 15 percent to 5.8 million. The number of business tax returns, which includes sole practitioners and part-time businesses, hit almost 25 million in 1999. Meanwhile, researchers studying entrepreneurship estimated that close to one in every twenty-five adults in the United States was actively trying to start his or her own business—"substantially more than the number of people who get married every year," says *Inc.* magazine.[14] The collapse of the dot-com bubble in mid-2000 and the ensuing economic downturn brought a screeching, but temporary, halt to this phenomenon. The drop in demand for Internet services, telecom, and related technology businesses led to massive layoffs. However, reports from northern California and other "new economy" bastions suggest that while there was some migration back into traditional organizations (where possible) many of these entrepreneurs viewed the recessionary trend as cyclical. They either returned to school to finish the educations they had interrupted to ride the tech wave or simply determined to wait the nine to twelve months estimates suggested it might take for the economy to revive. By late 2001, there were already reports of nascent revivals in selected areas like chip design, network security (an outgrowth of the terrorist attacks of September 11, 2001), and biotechnology.

Feeding this optimism about the economy's love affair with entrepreneurship are several factors: (1) more and more people are learning the skills of entrepreneurship, often in the same business schools that once prepared their students only for corporate careers. "It's like tennis—I can't guarantee how good you'll be if you take a course," a professor at the University of Southern California's Marshall School of Business told *Inc.*, describing his school's entrepreneurship courses. "But we can pretty much get you up to speed. We can provide the skill sets"[15]; (2) the recognition that there is a chronic shortage of innovative but commercially viable ideas to fuel economic growth. The dot-com bubble underscored the dangers of ignoring the emphasis on commercial viability, but companies continued to scan the horizon for growth prospects even in the depth of the downturn; and (3) availability of capital, both organized venture capital investments for fledgling companies with broad market potential and informal or "angel" venture capital for smaller ventures has fueled entrepreneurial activity. In 1999 researchers found that about 7 percent of U.S. adults had invested in some kind of start-up business. It wasn't much money, on average—only a few thousand dollars apiece. But those informal investments added up to an estimated total of $54 billion.[16] Again, the downturn that began in early 2000 had, a year later, reduced venture capital and angel investing by as much as 80 percent off its late-1999 highs (an angel investor is a high-net-worth individual interested in investing for his/her own account outside of the institutional market). However, the venture-capital industry acknowledged that it was imply returning to its saner, pre-bubble standards, not giving up on investing in new ventures.

The proliferation of small companies and upstarts in nearly every industry is a phenomenon that feeds on itself: the more there are, the more legitimacy they earn. No one can argue anymore that the most talented people all work for big companies. No big company can argue that it can afford to ignore smaller competitors.

Customer Expectations

In a preindustrial economy, people make what they need and buy what they can, and they count themselves lucky if they have adequate food, clothing, and shelter. In an industrial economy, people buy mass-produced goods—appliances, cars, ready-made clothing, and so on—and count themselves lucky because they can afford a standard of living well beyond what their parents and grandparents enjoyed. Today, expectations have ratcheted upward another couple of steps. Most consumers in developed nations take it for granted that they will have a reasonably comfortable standard of living, and they are no longer satisfied with standardized goods sold at reasonable prices. Some want small luxuries, such as a grande latte from Starbucks. Others want (and can afford) big luxuries, such as a Lexus automobile. Still others want products tailored to very specific wants and preferences—organically grown strawberries, authentic parts for vintage cars, fragrance-free, bleach-alternative detergent, CDs of sixteenth-century music recorded on period instruments. Suddenly products have proliferated almost beyond measure, even as buyers and sellers on sites such as eBay establish thousands of tiny marketplaces in which to trade specialized wares.

But it isn't just expectations of product diversity that have increased. In business and consumer markets alike, virtually everyone expects near-perfect manufacturing quality, along with speed and responsiveness in customer service. Many customers also expect certain kinds of ethical behavior on the part of the companies they deal with—not just honesty in business dealings, but (for example) a concern for the environment or for their employees.

THE EFFECTS OF THE CHANGE

What a transformation! Just to describe the series of changes is to underline how different things are today. In our economy, no big company anywhere in the world can assume that it can do business tomorrow the way it did in the past. There is too much uncertainty; there are too many competitive threats. Large corporations from other countries—with different management systems and different cost structures—continue to muscle in on one another's turf, threatening the very survival of the incumbents. Young, entrepreneurial businesses utilize new technologies to challenge even the best-established giants head-on. The continuing revolution in computer technology forces companies to update their information systems and reinvent themselves to take advantage of the new capabilities—or lose out to competitors who move faster. The rise of the service economy means that sheer size doesn't have the clout it once did. (If you're running a midsize manufacturing company would you rather deal with a giant money-center bank or a smaller, more personal bank?) Indeed, size can be a liability these days as well as an asset, since most large companies are notoriously slow to adapt to changing market conditions.

All these trends, in other words, seriously and substantially ratcheted up the level and the pace of competition. The effect can be seen in virtually every marketplace. Some markets are simply chaotic, like California's newly deregulated electric-power industry in 2001. Others are competitive to the point of destructiveness, like the personal-computer business. There are still plenty of globe-straddling giant companies—think of Citigroup, AOL Time Warner, and Microsoft, not to mention IBM and Toyota and Royal Dutch Shell. But is it really a sure thing that any one of them will be on top of its industry (or industries) in, say, ten years? You'd need a strong stomach to put all your money on that bet. And not one of these giants is acting complacent; on the contrary, they're all investing huge amounts of money in trying to maintain and solidify their positions of leadership. Like virtually every other businessperson today, their leaders understand the essential truth of the intangibles economy. No company can stand still. If it does, a competitor will leave it in the dust.

This increase in the level of competition, in turn, has increased the strategic importance of intangibles. If a company faces constant competition, after all, what does it have to fall back on? Size alone isn't enough. Physical assets—factories, stores, equipment—can help, but only until someone changes the rules of the game. Financial strength is always a plus, but it doesn't necessarily translate into competitive advantage. The major players in the global economy don't suffer from lack of access to resources. Thanks to the venture-capital market, even upstarts are likely to have plenty of cash at their disposal. What companies *can* fall back on are precisely those assets and competencies that are hardest for competitors to emulate: an ability to innovate—to come out regularly with new products and services; adaptability, or the ability to turn on a dime as market conditions change; dedicated, loyal, well-trained employees, along with leaders who are capable of inspiring them; a powerful brand (as important now as ever); a sterling reputation (more important than ever); and systems—information systems, production systems, service-delivery systems—that can provide customers what they want when they want it, with a bare minimum of problems or delays.

The key sources of value creation have also shifted from the tangible to the intangible. We see evidence of this both in the financial markets and in investment patterns. In 1997, for the first time since such figures were recorded, U.S. corporate investments in a set of intangibles (brand, training, and R&D) surpassed investments in the classic tangibles of property, plant, and equipment. The correlation between stock-price performance and traditional balance-sheet and income-statement measures has dramatically declined; yet the correlation between intangibles and stock-price performance can be measured with increasing accuracy, as our research shows. Why so? In effect, the forces producing the rise in the value and importance of intangibles—technology, globalization, and so on—also lead to an inability to sustain competitive advantage. The speed and connectivity of the global economy force managers to make bigger decisions with less information in shorter periods of time. Success in such a volatile and uncertain environment doesn't stem from historical factors, all neatly gathered, categorized, and studied. Rather, it's dependent on managerial competence—on factors like intelligence, leadership, and execution. Whatever competitive advantage may remain lies in intangibles.

So a second effect of all those trends is that *management* of an enterprise has become more and more important. Since this is a book about management as well as about intangibles, it's worth reviewing how this, too, changed dramatically in the past couple of decades.

In the industrial economy, relatively few corporate executives went to business school or read books about management. They learned their trade on the job; they stayed with one company for most of their careers. Neither the companies themselves nor the competitive landscape changed much over time, so managers didn't have to learn many new tricks. Business schools in those days were perceived as little more than training academies, suitable for students whose career aspirations didn't extend beyond making money. Management itself was scarcely perceived as a discipline; it was just running a company.

But the new economic environment brought equally new attitudes toward management. When Japanese manufacturers successfully attacked U.S. and European competitors, for instance, students of management traced their success to the way Japanese executives ran their companies. Terms such as *kaizen* and "quality circles" began to be bandied about. Television networks ran specials with titles such as "Why the U.S. Can't Compete," complete with film of Japanese employees doing early-morning calisthenics and singing the company song. To U.S. and European eyes, the tools and techniques their own managers had always relied on suddenly seemed inadequate to the task at hand.

As if in response, consultants Thomas J. Peters and Robert H. Waterman, Jr., published a book in 1982 arguing that U.S. companies *could* compete, but that they had to start doing things differently. That book, *In Search of Excellence*, became a world-class best-seller. What Peters and Waterman prescribed was a series of practical approaches to managing, cleverly labeled with homey headings like "management by walking around" or "stick to the knitting." The Peters and Waterman homilies suggested that the secret, if there was one, already resided in the skill set of the typical manager, and all he or she had to do was liberate it. No special sauce, just good old American know-how.

In Search of Excellence sparked a tidal wave of business-advice books. While this had always been a solid category in publishing, past titles tended to be how-to books, the memoirs of famous CEOs, or inspirational tomes by professional sports figures. Peters and Waterman identified a market for people who could write about ideas—about the philosophy of management. Peter Drucker, who had been writing about management ideas and practices for nearly forty years, suddenly became something of a celebrity; his books too hit the best-seller lists. Newer thinkers such as Charles Handy, Stephen Covey, and Peter Senge contributed ideas of their own. In effect, the explosion of books and the rise to prominence of the "business guru" signaled that the pressures of the 1970s and '80s had given impetus to new levels of intellectual curiosity and practical inquiry into the art of management.

What did it all mean? One conclusion was that managers had created a huge market for advice about how to manage better *and* about how to manage their role as manager. Management had finally become a profession separate from the functional specialties of human resources or finance or engineering, and separate from industry-specific specializations created around steel-rolling mills, direct-mail marketing, or software design. What's more, management *mattered*. Readers flocked to the new advice books (and to the speeches, conferences, and seminars that accompanied them) precisely because they knew that what they did on the job, every day, was one big factor in determining the success of their organization, not to mention their own personal success. In fact, the growth of any business now seemed to depend on better performance from leaders at all levels of the organization. Most significantly, these books all rocketed to the top of the charts, becoming best-sellers and racking up numbers that no previous generation of business books had ever seen. They also stood the test of time; subsequent editions have continued to sell, as have similar works produced by later writers. Yet none of them were about hard, functional topics such as how to set up a chart of accounts or how to sell real estate. They were all about intangibles.

So what managers learned from all these practical philosophers was that better performance turned on better understanding of intangibles. It was no longer enough just to practice the business-school catechism of managing the financials. Managers who did only that were steering the ship by looking at the wake. They couldn't even see the icebergs that might lie on the horizon. What mattered now were soft, hard-to-define notions like reputation and employee loyalty and an organization's ability to learn. Paying attention to these would enable the company to stay on top of the marketplace, to negotiate through treacherous straits, to avoid those icebergs. If intangibles had mattered in the past, and surely they did, they mattered much more now. Companies in this economy—the Intangibles Economy—don't just utilize intangible assets, as companies always have. Rather, they live or die on their ability to create invisible advantage from intangibles. That was the new job of management, and a tough one it would be.

DECODING THE
INTANGIBLES ECONOMY

*Over time, and particularly during the last decade or
two, an ever-increasing share of GDP has reflected
the value of ideas more than material substance or
manual labor input.*

—Alan Greenspan, Chairman
Federal Reserve Bank of the United States[1]

An economy in which intangibles loom so large presents a puzzle.
Economists don't really know what's going on, because the measurements they rely on capture only a portion of economic activity.
Accountants can give only a partial picture of a company's health, because they haven't yet developed tools to track and value assets that
can't be touched or spent. Investors are operating in the twilight. We
have found in our research that the savviest among them rely heavily
on intangibles in evaluating a company's performance and prospects
(which all by itself should be enough to make a CEO sit up and take
notice). But they don't do so systematically—and most companies
haven't yet figured out how to tell investors what they really need to
know.

So sit tight. This chapter will take up the noisy clamor for new metrics, fuller disclosure, and better information—and will show just
how important intangibles are in our new economic environment.

ECONOMISTS: THE (CLOUDY) BIG PICTURE

Every now and then you read an announcement of some new macroeconomic number, such as economic growth during the last quarter or the latest rate of inflation. Governments issue all kinds of economic statistics on a regular basis, and economists and businesspeople alike use these numbers as a guide for understanding where the economy has been and where it is headed. Of course, savvy statistics-watchers know that these numbers are only approximations. There's no way an economy as large and complex as that of the United States or any other industrial nation can be accurately tracked down to the last dollar. Still, most of the approximations—in the past, at least—have been pretty good. When the government said that economic growth was slowing or unemployment rising, people could usually notice the difference in everyday indicators like weekly sales or the size of the help-wanted sections.

But what if the statistics that purport to show economic activity actually miss a lot of it? At least a few well-respected economists argue that's exactly what has happened in recent years. The reason: intangibles.

One question, for example, is the degree to which companies are investing in intangibles, because these numbers don't show up on their income statements. As an economic adviser from the Philadelphia Fed, Leonard Nakamura uses three different techniques to come up with an estimate for this figure in the United States. His conclusion: Gross investment in intangibles totals a whopping $1 trillion per year, or very nearly the same amount U.S. companies invest in plant and equipment. Interestingly, Nakamura shows that investment in intangibles as a percent of GDP—in other words, compared to the size of the American economy—was pretty stable between 1959 and 1978, then rose sharply upward. The period after 1979 roughly corresponds to the economic sea change described in the previous chapter. Today, says Nakamura, actual GDP may be 10 percent higher than the government says it is, simply because intangibles such as "designs, software, blueprints, ideas, artistic expressions, and so on" aren't accurately counted.[2]

Similarly, Erik Brynjolffson, a professor at Massachusetts Institute of Technology's Sloan School of Business and codirector of MIT's Center for eBusiness, has studied a variety of data in an attempt to understand some statistical puzzles of the post-1970s economy. The puzzles themselves don't need to concern us here, but Brynjolffson's conclusions are germane indeed. Essentially, what he finds is that companies investing in computerization or new information-technology (IT) systems simultaneously invest much more in intangibles such as software, human capital (training, skill development), new business processes, and new organizational capabilities. Speaking to a 2001 conference on intangibles, Brynjolfsson cited the example of a company in the financial-services industry that had invested $800,000 in new computer hardware and a whopping $20.5 million more in accompanying intangibles. "These are real investments," said Brynjolffson, "as real as a new factory," but only the hardware shows up as assets on the balance sheet. Overall, he argues, the U.S. economy is creating more output than is captured in conventional statistics, precisely because of this investment in intangibles. "It's like a whole bunch of invisible factories," he concludes.[3]

Alan Greenspan would agree. Economists need to figure out how to measure and analyze the output of our increasingly complex economy, he said in the speech quoted at the top of this chapter. That, he added, would likely produce more benefits than building more and more complex computer models that try to predict our economic future.[4]

ACCOUNTANTS AND INVESTORS: THE PUSH FOR BETTER REPORTING

If economists are concerned that they're not counting GNP accurately, accountants sound as if they're beginning to get desperate. Listen to a sampling of the reports and pronouncements just from the last year or two:

- Even before the Enron disaster, which began to unfold as this book was going to press, Federal Reserve Board Chairman Alan Greenspan complained that accounting wasn't tracking investments in knowledge assets like the value of R&D, most software and brand equity and warned, 'There are going to be a lot of problems in the future.' Actually problems are here now. Former SEC Chairman Arthur Levitt told the Economic Club of New York, 'As intangible assets grow in size and scope, more and more people are questioning whether the true value—and the drivers of that value—are being reflected in a timely manner in publicly available disclosure.'"[5]

- A task force appointed by the U.S. Securities and Exchange Commission urged the SEC in May 2001 to "encourage" companies to provide more information on intangible assets. "The kind of information that is needed is not provided by traditional accounting methods," said Jeffrey E. Garten, task force chair and dean of the Yale School of Management. Added task force member (and leading venture capitalist) John Doerr, using the well-known acronym for Generally Accepted Accounting Principles: "There is a gap in GAAP."[6] Meanwhile, the Financial Accounting Standards Board (FASB) 2001 special report *Business and Financial Reporting, Challenges from the New Economy* says, "Improved business and financial reporting of the 'new economy' will require attention to recognition of internally generated intangible assets in financial statements and improved measures of those assets."[7]

- The Institute for Chartered Accountants in England and Wales (ICAEW) has released a string of reports on intangibles in the last few years. For example, the ICAEW proposal entitled *The 21st Century Annual Report* questioned whether "traditional audited financial statements take sufficient account of. . . intangible assets . . ." and asked "are we discriminating against intangibles in our accounting system since the valuation of properties, work in progress and provisions for doubtful debts, to name but three, can also be very subjective?"[8]

- The European Commission's High-Level Expert Group in their 2000 report "The Intangible Economy—Impact and Policy Issues" says, "Far from being new topics, knowledge and intangibles have been important throughout history. The difference is that, today, a firm's intangible assets are often the key element in its competitiveness. Increasingly, the capacity to combine external and internal sources of knowledge to exploit commercial opportunities has become a distinctive competency." The report goes on to say, "The impact of knowledge and intangibles will be greater for old-established companies than for dot-coms and other 'new economy' enterprises" and concludes with the statement, "The present economic, statistical and accounting frameworks are in urgent need of updating. New explanatory models and metrics are needed to enable us to understand the workings of the modern economy, especially the intangible goods and 'content' sectors that are currently hidden from public view."[9]

Whew! And this isn't even the end of the story. On the academic front, accounting theorists such as New York University's Baruch Lev are working on creating new kinds of financial statements designed to capture the value of intangible capital. FASB, the SEC, and the

European Commission have themselves conducted studies and issued reports on new ways of approaching intangible assets. Meanwhile, think tanks such as The Brookings Institution, the Conference Board, and the American Enterprise Institute have put task forces to work and also have begun issuing reports. (In 2001, Brookings published *Unseen Wealth* by Margaret M. Blair and Steven M. H. Wallman, who had cochaired the institution's task force on intangibles.) In Europe, the European Commission issued a Request for Proposals in the summer of 2001 to study measurement of intangibles and develop related policy proposals. It is funding additional research on these issues, as are most of the major European governments. The Organization for Economic Cooperation and Development (OECD) is considering the creation of a committee to design principles for the disclosure of intangibles. Meanwhile, companies themselves are devoting more and more effort to the development of nonfinancial performance measures—rates of innovation, time to market, employee satisfaction, and so on. Many are issuing addenda to their annual reports that focus on their performance on such measures.

What's going on here, of course, is pretty simple: Nearly everybody realizes that *financial statements, despite the precision with which they are prepared, are illusory*. As the Enron case makes clear, they don't accurately reflect a company's performance, let alone its prospects for the future. Indeed, the gap between market value and book value—indicated by the so-called market-to-book ratio—has been rising more or less steadily since the early 1980s, a trend that by itself suggests the growing importance of intangibles. (The one intangible that is reflected in financial statements—goodwill— usually obscures as much as it illuminates, and as this book goes to press the accounting rules governing goodwill are about to change.[10]) Everyday accountants and financial analysts are thus faced with vexing problems. When Amazon.com went into the bond market a couple of years ago, for example, Wall Street was uncertain how to price the bonds, because the company had so little in the way of tangible assets to back them up.[11] During the dot-com craze, Wall Street invented a variety of methods for evaluating Internet companies' performance. Unfortunately, virtually none of them were based on credible analysis—and none of them proved accurate. Market valuations suggest that intangibles are valuable—and growing more so—but unless they are carefully thought through, we don't know *how* valuable or *why* they are valuable.

MEASURES THAT MATTER

To shed some light on these questions, we want to turn to research that we and our colleagues conducted at the Cap Gemini Ernst & Young Center for Business Innovation (CBI). If you have any doubt about the power of intangibles to affect the value of a company, this research should put your doubts to rest.

We know who assesses the book value of a business: accountants. But who assesses a company's market value? Ultimately, of course, it's the market itself—thousands or maybe millions of investors, each making up his or her own mind about what a stock is worth. But some among this crowd are more influential than others. They are the professional investors, the denizens of Wall Street and its counterparts around the world, the people who spend full time analyzing companies and making multimillion-dollar investment decisions every day on behalf of big institutions and mutual funds. These individuals' reputations, compensation, and careers rise and fall with their investment choices. They have a lot at stake in getting things right. So do the employees and managers of the businesses they cover, who suffer when the investors get it wrong for whatever reason.

In the not-too-distant past, the job of a professional investor or investment analyst was essentially to crunch the numbers. To be sure, he or she would make a point of talking to a company's management, its customers, and its suppliers to get a handle on its business plans and prospects. Gut feeling about the company was always important.

But what the analyst really wanted to know was what the financials showed last year or last quarter, and what they were likely to show in the upcoming quarter. The pros scrutinized income statements, balance sheets, and cash-flow statements. They looked at a company's size, its market share, its debt-to-equity ratio, and other easy-to-measure indicators of financial strength. They based their earnings estimates and their buy-or-sell recommendations mostly on the tangible and the countable.

But in the 1990s, things were changing. Academics had begun to realize that intangible assets were increasingly important in our economy, and that financial statements alone weren't necessarily the best guide to a company's future. Wall Street, and the financial professionals who provide it with information, began asking whether they themselves really had all the information they needed. As far back as 1991, a committee of the American Institute of Certified Public Accountants—the so-called Jenkins Committee—issued a report recommending that corporations be encouraged to provide more "forward-looking information," and that they offer "enhanced discussion of the nonfinancial performance factors that create longer-term value."[12] This was sober and understated, as befits a committee of CPAs, but it was what passes for a bombshell in the world of accounting. (Look at *nonfinancial* performance factors? Wow!) Two years later, the Association for Investment Management and Research released a position paper espousing similar views. "For financial analysts to make sound judgments and draw rational conclusions, they must judge the performance of individual business enterprises . . . ," the paper said. "To do so, they need information of two types. First, management should explicitly describe its strategies, plans, and expectations. Much of this must come in the form of narrative descriptive material."[13]

So there were straws of change in the wind, but their significance was hard to assess. At the CBI, we and our colleagues began to study the growing importance of intangibles, and we wondered about the effect of such recommendations. Were Wall Street analysts and investors really beginning to scrutinize nonfinancial measures? Were they getting—and paying attention to—"narrative descriptive material"? If so, how important was all this nonfinancial data in determining share prices and thus company valuations? The research project that came to be called *Measures That Matter*, which we and our colleagues at the CBI conducted, was designed to answer these questions. It unfolded over three phases.

Phase One was essentially information gathering. This was five years ago, and at the time there was no common language or framework for talking about intangibles. We didn't know what nonfinancial information might be important to investors, or how they might use the information that they got. So we started out simply by listening. We interviewed portfolio managers. We talked to experts on intangibles. In Phase Two we gathered up some 300 investment reports prepared by the people Wall Street calls sell-side analysts. Sell-side analysts work for investment houses. Their job is to follow particular industries and companies, issue reports on the companies' operations and prospects, and ultimately make recommendations as to whether investors should buy, hold, or sell the stocks in question. We wanted to know a few things about the reports they issue: whether and how the analysts utilized nonfinancial data in these reports, and whether there was any correlation between their use of this information and the accuracy of their earnings forecasts. (There's more on sell-side analysts—and the controversies surrounding them—in chapter seven.)

The results of this research phase were compelling. *Nearly all the analysts relied heavily on a broad range of intangible factors to make their decisions.* They looked at companies' capabilities in customer retention and marketing. They assessed internal factors such as production efficiency, employee empowerment, and incentive compensation. Most powerful of all, we found, was the high correlation between analysts' use of such data and the accuracy of their forecasts. The more that an analyst took nonfinancial factors into account, the more accurate were his or her earnings predictions.

Still, the role of an analyst is only advisory. Analysts themselves don't make investment decisions. To see whether intangibles really affected financial outcomes like share prices and market cap, we wanted to ask whether investment professionals themselves actually used intangible factors in determining which companies to invest in.

This part of the study was the heart of our research. In it, we surveyed so-called buy-side investors, the people who manage portfolios for pension and mutual funds, bank and insurance-company wealth-management businesses, and other large financial institutions. These institutions have typically controlled about 70 percent of the outstanding shares of most publicly traded companies, and the individuals who manage their portfolios make decisions that go a long way toward establishing a company's value in the capital markets. We asked respondents to tell us how important information about intangibles was to their investment decisions. We asked, for example, what percentage of their investment decisions were based on nonfinancial data. We listed thirty-nine types of nonfinancial data—everything from "new product-development cycle time" to "environmental and social policies"—and asked the investors to rank their importance. We also asked them to rank the value of different data sources.

The next part of the survey took a different approach. Rather than asking for opinions, we presented our respondents with hypothetical stock-purchase scenarios. Here's how it worked:

First, we listed four industries—computer hardware, oil and gas exploration and production, food processing, and pharmaceuticals—and four companies within each industry. Each respondent got a "fund" to allocate among the industries and companies. We gave them a set of financial performance data, including price/earnings ratios, sales growth rates, and earnings per share. We also provided information on nonfinancial performance, divided into eight categories. Once the respondents had allocated their fund among the sixteen possible choices, our statisticians were able to deduce each investor's actual preference for particular performance indicators.

Next, respondents were presented with four different financial scenarios for each set of companies. The financial results were new, but the nonfinancial indicators remained unchanged. We then asked the investors to reallocate their funds, and we observed how their decisions changed. Again, statistical techniques allowed us to assess the relative importance of various financial and nonfinancial indicators.

These conclusions weren't just compelling, they were downright startling. About seven out of every ten of these hard-nosed Wall Street pros said that nonfinancial data drove at least 30 percent of their investment decisions. When we analyzed what professional investors actually did, as opposed to what they said, we came up with a firmer number: on average, 35 percent of professional investors' allocation decisions are driven by consideration of nonfinancial data or information about intangibles. In other words, *more than one-third of the information used to justify these large-scale investment decisions is nonfinancial.*

Not surprisingly, every respondent had his or her own hierarchy. Information about strategy execution, management credibility, and innovation tended to be far more important than measures of customer complaints, employee-training programs, or environmental and social policies. Also not surprisingly, the importance of various intangibles varied from one industry to another. In computers, quality of management was the single most important factor in these investors' minds. In oil and gas, companies gained value not only from strong management but from strong supplier relations and distribution channels. In pharmaceuticals, the biggest single factor was quality of new-product development. Later in this book we'll help you assess which particular intangible assets matter most for various industries.

Right now, though, reflect on the basic conclusion. In effect, about a third of these investors' buying and selling decisions are determined by nonfinancial information—information to which managers often give scarcely a second thought. While the people who run companies are busy beefing up their balance sheets and managing their earnings, the people who invest in companies are looking at indicators such as what's in the R&D pipeline, whether the company has the talent it needs, and whether it does what it says it's going to do.

In short: the market is evaluating your company right now, day in and day out, on the basis of your intangibles—and market participants may not be asking for your opinion about how they reach their conclusions. You and your executive team may not be aware of this; you may not even be devoting explicit managerial attention to these intangibles. If that's the case, you're missing an opportunity to affect how the market values your stock.

It's true that neither economists nor accountants have good measures yet for evaluating intangibles, though that may soon begin to change. Even Wall Street tends to do it by guess and by golly. In the meantime, there's an opportunity here: to manage the very intangibles that matter, and to communicate what you do to the investing public. There is probably no other part of your business that you leave so much to chance, or to the decisions of others, without even attempting to participate in the conversation. Why would you fail to act when doing so can affect your most valuable financial asset—your stock price?

IPOs AND INTANGIBLES

The power of intangibles can be seen equally dramatically in an analysis of initial public offerings (IPOs).

Probably nothing captured the frenzied promise of the Internet revolution as much as these financial transactions. IPOs monetized the hopes and dreams of the entrepreneurs who thought they were creating a new economy. IPOs symbolized the promise and ultimately the disappointment of the Internet boom. Online grocer Webvan raised $375 million in its 1999 IPO, the stock rising from an opening price of $15 to a first-day high of $34. The company subsequently went bankrupt. Garden.com, though less ambitious, still brought in about $50 million from its 1999 IPO, and watched its stock rise from $12 to more than $19 on the first day alone. It shut its doors in late 2000. Nor was it just Internet stocks that partook of the bubble and the later devastation. Red Hat, a leader in open-source software, went from $14 to $52 on the first day of trading and eventually hit an incredible high of $151. In late 2001 it was selling below $4.

But the glamour and collapse of IPOs in the brief period 1999 through 2001 shouldn't blind us to the critically important role these transactions have played in the economy for many years now. In the last fifteen years as a whole—from 1986 to 2001—personal computing, biotechnology, software, telecommunications, the Internet, and a host of related products and services contributed to huge changes in the way companies do business and people live their lives. Many of the companies that pioneered these new technologies raised funds through an IPO. So did many innovative companies in low-tech industries such as retailing. In so doing they established a value for their enterprises, raised billions in various currencies to fund what they hoped would be continued growth, and created billions in personal wealth. An example of a successful IPO is the housewares chain Bed Bath & Beyond Inc., which went public in 1992. Since then both its revenues and its stock price have grown steadily, as its stock has considerably outperformed the S&P 500 since its IPO.

What do we find when we look at the performance of IPOs over time? You might think they would do well, given the excitement they always generate on Wall Street and their importance in the economy—except when there's a bubble such as that of the Internet. In fact IPOs typically do poorly. Companies going public for the first time underperform the market in both operating returns and share-price returns in the first three years. This finding was first documented by Jay Ritter, an economist at the University of Florida, in his study of IPOs from 1970 through the mid-1980s. It persists to this day, even through the strongest bull market in Wall Street history, that of the 1990s. But this is an observation that raises a host of questions. Why do so many IPOs do badly? Why should some enjoy stellar records when so many underperform the market? What separates the winners from the losers?

Hoping to answer just such questions, we and our colleagues at the CBI conducted research on the role of intangibles in the success of IPOs. The research—done in partnership with other CGEY colleagues and with academics from Harvard Business School and INSEAD— covered the period 1986 through 2001. We divided the IPOs during that time into three periods, roughly corresponding to the early PC and software era (1986–90), the era in which biotech and pharmaceutical companies predominated (1990–95), and the dot.com/Internet era that began with Netscape's IPO in 1995 and continued until the Nasdaq market crash in 2000.

Because we were interested in the "why" as well as the "what," we took a somewhat unusual approach. The financial markets usually define success purely in terms of share price and increase in *market capitalization* (number of shares times the share price). We chose also to ask executives who had been through an IPO during these eras how successful or unsuccessful they thought their IPO had been, and to what factors they attributed the result. Their responses were then compared with share-price and market-cap data; the goal was both to assess the accuracy of the responses and to enable CBI researchers to test the importance of the various factors noted by the executives. The study drew on a universe of 3,859 U.S. companies that had gone public between January 1, 1986, and December 31, 2000. Except for real-estate-investment trusts, warrants, ADRs and various untraceable companies, this included all of the companies that had gone public in the United States during that time frame. We received detailed questionnaires from senior executives of more than 480 of these companies; the response rate—13 percent—is above the norm for survey research.

Findings

The research provides a number of fascinating insights into intangibles and IPOs:

- IPOs as a rule do indeed perform relatively poorly;
- Intangibles are significant differentiators between IPOs that create value and those that do not;
- Intangibles are more important than traditional financial measures in determining an IPO's success or failure;
- The popular perception that successful IPOs are based, most importantly, on technology, is largely a myth; the factors that differentiated successful from unsuccessful IPOs were fairly consistent over the fifteen years we studied and had more to do with intangibles like strategy, leadership, alliances, and adaptability.
- Had proper attention been paid to these intangibles, investors might not have lost so much money, employees might not have lost their jobs, and more of these companies might have survived.

Let's look at some of the findings in more detail.

First, throughout the period studied—the period of greatest equity wealth creation in history—the "typical" IPO company was older and had more employees than you might think. Three nerdy guys who had spent a year in a northern California garage? Hardly: Forty-six percent of the IPOs were at least eleven years old at the time of the offering, with over a quarter having been in business for more than twenty years. Eighty percent had at least 100 employees, and 36 percent had more than 500 employees. The importance of such information is confirmed by data on the stocks held by investment banks underwriting IPOs. Underwriters held stock in 80 percent of the older, more established IPOs but held stock in only 20 percent of the younger companies.

Second, the average age of the companies going public decreased from twenty-one to ten years during the period studied. Ten years is still appreciably older than the perceived—and actual—age of many dot.coms. But what's striking is the correlation between the decline in average age and size of IPOs over the fifteen-year period and the decline in the percentage of IPOs that created value during that period. During the first two periods analyzed, between 30 and 40 percent of the companies going public failed to gain market value after one year. By the end of the dot-com era, between 1996 and 2000, more than 55 percent were failing to do so. The two-year and three-year results indicate an even higher rate of failure by this criterion. And lest there be any question about the cost of an unsuccessful IPO, our research shows that the difference in market value per enterprise between an IPO rated highly successful by its executives and one rated unsuccessful averaged $126 million in the first period and $1.01 billion in the dot-com period.

The implication: Intangibles such as experience (reflected in the age and scope of the enterprise) matter to IPO success rates. In fact, a majority of the companies surveyed noted that they wished they had engaged in a strategic acquisition *before* they went public to beef up their balance sheet and income statement.

The implications were most stark in the case of dot-com enterprises; what we heard from dot-com CEOs corresponded with the statistical results. The human capital represented by the intelligence and enthusiasm they brought to their new enterprises could get them only so far. They needed the full basket or web of intangibles—intangibles such as alliances, culture, reputation, and strategy execution—to realize their full potential. Process factors, functional factors, and competitive factors must all be present to meet the promise inherent in the establishment of a brand. Interestingly, much of the hype in the business press portrayed dot-coms as savvy and successful in their intangibles-based performance—they hired smart people, made solid strategic alliances, established first-mover advantage—yet survey results show that dot-coms were actually doing worse than their more traditional competitors on such measures.

The divergent experiences of garden.com and Webvan, on the one hand, and Bed Bath & Beyond, on the other, are instructive in this regard. At both garden.com and Webvan, efforts to install financial and operational systems were inadequate. Both were notable for failures of customer service, perhaps reflecting the common dot-com notions that advertising equals brand building, and that if you build it, they— the customers—will come. Customers might have come once, but few come again after an unsatisfying experience. Brand is a promise to the customer, and failure to deliver on that promise can be fatal. Also, even though Webvan did make a large acquisition after its IPO, the acquisition was ineffectively integrated, thereby sowing operational confusion and customer dissatisfaction. That compounded another of the company's fundamental problems, namely a business plan that offered no realistic hope of profitability.

By contrast, Bed Bath & Beyond concentrated on the customer experience as the logical focus of its strategy. It identified its market—middle-class home-improvement shoppers—and pursued it relentlessly, using all the marketing, advertising, display, locational, and promotional weapons at its disposal. The important difference here isn't that between the Web-based strategies of garden.com and Webvan and the bricks-and-mortar strategy of Bed Bath & Beyond. Rather, the difference is one of outlook and execution. Bed Bath & Beyond was not captivated by the romance or buzz associated with its business, limited though that may be. It concentrated on building its brand by delivering a positive customer experience and continually reinvesting in enhancements to that experience (or in growth opportunities related to it).

Implications

The size of the financial incentive described above makes it imperative that executives in companies going public do everything they can to do it well. Our research demonstrates that intangible factors are more likely than traditional financial factors to lead to a successful public offering. The lessons:

Treat the IPO like a transformation, not just a transaction.   Changing from private or corporate ownership to public ownership is a conversion that requires more than just superficial changes. The expectations and demands of everyone involved with the company, from employees and customers to investors and lenders, will be different.

Prepare for the transformation. Upgrade or replace programs, policies, and systems covering information technology, compensation plans, organizational design, boards of directors, financial accounting, and reporting systems. The goal is to act like a public company before becoming one. Our research showed that this was one crucial determinant of success.

Beef up your competitive position. The highly successful companies surveyed were not just strong competitors; their executives ranked them significantly stronger than their public competitors along all financial and nonfinancial factors at the time of the offering. If you're considering an IPO, ask yourself whether you can do the same. If not, consider revamping your strategies for acquisitions and financings.

Allow sufficient lead time. Most executives surveyed felt they were not adequately prepared to go public. Those that began revamping their internal systems between one and two years prior to the offering earned significantly higher returns than those who waited until later. Unlike the executives who reported unsuccessful offerings, 49 percent of whom never made strategic changes, 66 percent of those who reported successful offerings had plans in place before going to market.

Listen to your shareholders. Companies with venture-capital backing (a distinct minority, which shatters another myth) told us that they wished they had paid more intention to their VCs and less to the blandishments of investment bankers, whose financial incentive was to get the deal done rather than to look out for the company's best long-term interests. In fact, an interesting feature of the dot-com period was that those who cited *more* worries about what their competitors were doing before the IPO did worse than executives who worried less about competitors. The go-public-because-my-competitors-are-doing-so IPOs appear to have been destined to fail.

Make sure your "people" systems are in place.   The most significant intangible differentiator was driven by human capital. The old bankers' cliché—"we don't invest in companies, we invest in people"—turns out to be a useful guide. Retention of current employees was frequently mentioned as a primary motivation for the IPO. Improvements in employee-incentive programs, made by 57 percent of all respondents, appear to have had a greater impact on the company's subsequent performance *than any of the seventeen other policies and practices cited.*

These findings shed some light on both the dot-com bubble and the Nasdaq collapse. Many of the factors cited as important to IPO success declined dramatically from 1986 to 2000. In effect, the companies that went public between the Netscape IPO in 1995 and the last gasp of the IPO frenzy in early 2000 were inherently weaker than many of their predecessors. It's no exaggeration to say that, based on these criteria, they were destined to fail. But what's interesting here is that the data were available before the dot-com bubble. IPOs were known to be risky; trends in the quality of the companies being taken public were deteriorating. The results, for which the global economy was still paying in the autumn of 2001, support the dark side of intangibles in this allegedly rational modern age: Belief systems trump information systems. While a lot of fingers have been pointed at securities analysts, the financial press, investment bankers, and VCs, the comic strip character Pogo's famous dictum probably says it best: "We have met the enemy, and he is us." Many people knew what was coming, because the trends identifying their behavior were so clear. However, knowledge does not appear to have saved many people from "the greater fool theory" of behavior—that someone with less perfect knowledge would buy their shares for more than they paid and make them rich before the market turned.

The IPO phenomenon is a microcosm of a larger transformation: the increasing importance of the adaptive enterprise and of successful organizational transitions in effecting that adaptation so that the growth and sustainability of the corporate enterprise can be sustained or renewed. Such a transition can be a merger, acquisition, divestiture, or IPO. What the research shows is that intangibles play a significant role in differentiating between transitions that create wealth and those that destroy it.

PART TWO

The Twelve Intangibles That Drive Performance

MANAGING INTANGIBLES:
AN OVERVIEW

The rest of this book is about the ground-level, nitty-gritty challenge of managing your company's intangibles.

From our own research and that of others, we have identified twelve key clusters of intangibles, devoting a chapter in this section to the challenges and opportunities of managing each one. Our list is a little longer than many such lists (because we wanted to err on the side of inclusiveness, and also because we believe these are such critical drivers). Plenty of writers focus on what they call intellectual capital, for instance, and forget the issue of whether a company actually has a strategy that it can execute. Or they concentrate on human capital—the acquisition and retention of raw talent—while ignoring the workplace culture that encourages or discourages the application of talent to the job at hand. Since every industry is different, you'll inevitably find some chapters that are more relevant to your own situation than others.

Still, managers cannot afford to skip any of these twelve clusters entirely. The reason is simple: Taken together, these are the intangibles that drive a company's value in today's marketplace. Astute management of these drivers is what can make the difference between a market leader and an also-ran.

What are the issues involved in managing intangibles effectively? The chapters will (each) go into detail on this question, but it may be helpful to offer a few preliminary observations, if only because intangibles have many traits in common. They present a similar set of difficulties, and they offer a similar set of opportunities—opportunities that often exist precisely because managing intangibles is hard. Consider just a few of each.

INTANGIBLES LET YOU MANAGE IN REAL TIME— AND ANTICIPATE PROBLEMS BEFORE THEY ARISE.

Look only at your company's financial performance and you're looking in the rearview mirror: You can see what you did last month or last year, but not what's coming down the road. Intangibles help you understand how you're doing right now and learn how you're likely to do next year. In one widely discussed example, Sears, Roebuck & Company developed measurements of employee satisfaction, and tracked the relationship between this metric, customer loyalty, and financial performance. The company found that a 5-unit increase in employee attitude led to a 1.3-unit increase in "customer impression" (a variable related to customer retention), and that in turn drove a 0.5-percent increase in revenue growth.[1] More generally, Claes Fornell and researchers at the University of Michigan Business School's National Quality Research Center have produced since 1994 the American Customer Satisfaction Index (ACSI). The mathematical models contained in the index allow companies to measure customer satisfaction, point to areas for improvement, and demonstrate a clear link between customer satisfaction and financial metrics such as market value added (MVA), stock price, and return on investment.[2]

The trick here, of course, is to get metrics that accurately assess the intangibles critical to a business's success. How many companies feel truly comfortable with their measures of customer or employee satisfaction? How many even attempt to assign a value to their R&D efforts, let alone to the quality of their leadership? In our research, we asked a sample of executives in the financial services industry whether they were satisfied with their companies' measurements of nonfinancial performance indicators. The answer? No. On a one-to-six scale, the average level of satisfaction expressed by these executives barely topped three. In nearly every category, there were significant gaps between the *importance* executives attached to the intangibles (innovation, customer satisfaction) and the extent to which they actually tried to *measure* those intangibles. Even Sears was unable to maintain for more than two years the momentum identified by its initial research. Still, when the company's growth leveled off, its continuing efforts to pinpoint such values provided its managers with leads on how to rekindle growth.

When companies do learn to measure an intangible over time, what a difference it makes. Take quality. Twenty years ago, many U.S.-made goods—automobiles among them—were notoriously shoddy. New-car buyers literally expected that there would be a couple of dozen things wrong with the car they just bought, and that the dealer would have to fix them. Today that's no longer the case; defects are more the exception than the rule. The reason is that U.S. manufacturers have learned the techniques of measuring and analyzing quality pioneered (and first implemented in Japan) by innovators such as W. Edwards Deming and Joseph Juran. Once a factory begins utilizing statistical process control, root-cause analysis, and other tools for analyzing and maintaining quality levels, the intangible known as quality suddenly becomes susceptible to management. The state-of-the-art quality approach called Six Sigma, famously implemented at General Electric, is credited by former GE CEO Jack Welch with saving that company $12 billion over five years.

Like so many intangibles, quality is something you can manage now, as it is being determined. The payoffs are reflected in the financials, later.

INTANGIBLES HAVE FREQUENT— AND USUALLY POSITIVE—SPILLOVER EFFECTS.

This is a problem for conventional managerial thinking, which links activities to one another in sequential fashion. Intangibles affect each other in real time, and often they're all of a piece. Take as simple an example as Starbucks, which has built itself into a company with a $6.9-billion market cap and 5.45 market-to-book ratio (in mid-2001)—a valuable enterprise by anyone's definition, but particularly so for a company whose primary business is selling specialty coffee drinks. Does Starbucks's value come from the products themselves, from the ubiquity or ambiance of its restaurants, from the skills of its employees, from the ancillary products (coffee beans, mugs, etc.) it sells, or from the cachet produced by its marketing efforts? Obviously it's all of the above, and more besides. But each one reinforces the other. When Starbucks's Portland, Oregon, stores took part in the city's "Word on the Street" program celebrating literature and literacy, the stores were subtly (and simultaneously) building its brand, enhancing its reputation, and helping customers feel good about themselves for being the kind of people who would be drinking such a company's coffee.

Because of this interaction, improvement in one area can often lead to quite unexpected improvement in others. An example is Alcoa under Paul O'Neill. O'Neill—appointed in January 2001 as George W. Bush's first secretary of the treasury—took over the big aluminum producer in mid–1987, when it was (per *BusinessWeek*'s Michael Arndt) "just another wheezing industrial giant with an unremarkable financial record and a workforce that was biding its time." O'Neill set about shaking things up, but he didn't focus on customary measures like profit margins. Instead he drove a stake in the ground on workplace safety. Alcoa, he proclaimed, would be the safest company in its industry, measured by time lost to workplace accidents.

The result? Here is Arndt's account (in early 2001):

> *Alcoa's rate of time lost because of employee injuries was one-third the U.S. average when O'Neill took over. Today, it is less than one-twentieth. More important, O'Neill's emphasis on safety fundamentally altered Alcoa's culture. To meet his targets,*

managers and even bottom-rung workers began showing initiative instead of mutely waiting for orders. Productivity soon began rising, with a timely assist from the high-tech tools O'Neill also introduced, and then so did the financial tallies. . . .

Today, Alcoa is the global leader O'Neill envisioned. In 1986, the Pittsburgh-based company recorded $264 million in net income on sales of $4.6 billion; it had 35,700 employees and a market cap of $2.9 billion. When O'Neill retired at the end of 2000, at age sixty-five, Alcoa boasted record profits of $1.5 billion on sales of $22.9 billion and a payroll of 140,000. Meantime its market cap—up 126 percent in 1999 when Alcoa was the top stock among the thirty Dow Jones industrials—stands today at $29.9 billion.[3]

From February 2001 to November 2001, Alcoa's market cap rose from $29.9 billion to $32.1 billion.

Consider the interaction between reputation and other intangibles. The Hay Group, which produces the "Global Most Admired Companies" report for *Fortune* magazine, found that companies making the list "set more challenging goals, linked compensation . . . more closely to the completion of those goals and are generally more oriented toward long-term performance." In specific terms, "almost 60% of the Most Admired Companies rely on customer indicators like satisfaction, loyalty and market share. Only 38% of their peers do. And 40% of Most Admired Companies chart retention, career development, and other employee-oriented measurements; that's more than triple the percentage of companies that didn't make the list." BP Amoco, for instance, maps "qualitative performance measures such as innovation, mutual trust and respect, teamwork and diversity. . . . [It] recognizes that achievements in these areas are just as important to the success of the company as revenues, profits, and other financial measures."[4]

Investments in one intangible often *require* investments in others. This point is made in a report on intangibles prepared for the

Brookings Institution in 2000. "For example, investing in information technologies that deliver more and different information to people at the front lines without concurrently devolving authority and responsibility for decision making to them and without insuring that they understand strategic objectives might prove worse than making no investment at all. Playing the trade-off game with intangibles can seriously diminish or even negate desired results."[5]

THE VALUE OF AN INTANGIBLE CAN BE HUGE— MUCH MORE THAN ITS COST.

Investment in intangibles can pay off beyond any conventional ROI calculation. If a pharmaceutical company's R&D leads to a blockbuster new drug, or if a fashion house produces a hot new look, the rewards exceed the expenditures by orders of magnitude. But this opportunity doesn't apply only to industries that deal primarily in intellectual property. Take the money that Southwest Airlines spends to recruit, screen, and hire people who fit in with—and can contribute to—its good-time, go-get-'em culture. (In 1998 the company had 140,000 job applicants, interviewed about 90,000—and hired 4,200.) Add in what it spends to train its people and to spread the culture. Is it all worth it? We think it is. No doubt Southwest's people policies cost a lot, but the amount is tiny compared to the year-in, year-out profits that Southwest earns for its shareholders in a notoriously tough industry. At the end of September 2001, Southwest's price-to-sales ratio was 2.10, as compared with the airline-industry average of 1.35.

It's hard to calculate the value of an intangible. U.S. industry spent more than $177 billion in 2000 on R&D, only some of which will ever lead to marketable products.[6] Calculating a discounted cash flow analysis of a proposed investment in a tangible asset is a relatively straightforward process for a financial professional, and usually enough is known about the investment's likely payoff that managers can make reasonable decisions about whether it's worth the cost. But a similar analysis of a brand-awareness campaign or a corporate reorganization is likely to be a good deal more difficult, though every bit as worthwhile in the end.

. . . But that value is likely to be volatile

New York University Professor of Management at the Stern School of Business Charles Fombrun has shown that a single event—the widely publicized (though tiny) flaw in one of Intel's chips, for example, that occurred a few years ago—can knock billions of dollars off a company's market cap simply by damaging its reputation.[7] As we noted earlier, Coca-Cola lost $34 billion in market value after the Belgian children fell ill and claimed that the cause of their illness was tainted cans of Coke. And it's hard to know, as this book goes to press, what the ultimate outcome of the Firestone debacle will be. The allegations of defective tires mounted by Ford and others, whether or not they are eventually supported by impartial analysis, may wind up utterly destroying the historic brand.

Even in less calamitous circumstances, the intangible known as reputation can be tough to manage. When Nike set up its Web-site feature allowing customers to personalize their sneakers with distinctive colors and a 16-character message, an MIT graduate student named Jonah Peretti requested a pair of shoes labeled with the word "sweatshop," reflecting allegations that the company's overseas suppliers rely on oppressed low-wage labor. Nike was not amused, and responded with an e-mail detailing its rules for acceptable messages. Peretti replied that "sweatshop" didn't appear to break any of these rules. After a few more exchanges Nike ended the conversation with the declaration that the company doesn't print anything it doesn't want to. Peretti forwarded the e-mails to a few friends, and soon they were zipping their way around the globe. In March 2001 Peretti said he was receiving 500 e-mails a day from people vowing to boycott Nike's products. Nike, for its part, was devoutly hoping the story would quickly blow over.[8]

Yet intangibles such as reputation offer a giant opportunity on this front as well: They provide a company with a competitive edge that nobody else in the industry can just go out and buy. Southwest's culture, Toyota's "bulletproof quality," Johnson & Johnson's reputation for integrity (remember the famous Tylenol scare?), Dell Computer's ability to custom-design and manufacture a computer in a few days, Intel's technological leadership, General Electric's famed management-development systems—all these are invisible advantages that have been developed and cultivated over years. They are worth untold billions in the marketplace, yet no competitor can easily emulate them.

Once again, this is just a sampling—a foretaste—of the challenges and opportunities of managing intangibles. It's time now for specifics. The twelve chapters that follow are divided into three subsections. The first group focuses on a company's leadership—the quality of its management, and whether it can do what it says it will do. The second group focuses on external intangibles such as the company's reputation in the eyes of customers and the larger society. The third group examines what happens inside the organization. The concluding chapters—Part Three of the book—help you put it all together and figure out where to get started.

LEADERSHIP

*The way we teach leadership is to look at Leonardo
da Vinci in the Renaissance. He was not just design-
ing by himself, he always had 30 or 40 people around
him and they all learned from each other. So we get
people from different divisions to come together.
Every conversation becomes a case study.*

—Concetta Lanciaux, Group Executive
Vice President of Synergies, LVMH

The collapse of the equity markets in mid-2000 and the events of
September 11, 2001, amplified the pressures on leaders in every field
of endeavor. For the first time in almost a generation, the economic
downturn was global rather than regional, meaning that for the first
time since globalization became the corporate norm, there was no safe
haven from which sales and profits could be accumulated to offset the
troubles in some other region. In addition, the terrorist attacks on
New York and Washington, D.C., raised the notion of risk management from a quantifiable but frequently hypothetical exercise to a
common concern for basic physical safety. The reduction of financial
and personal security at one time—in all likelihood, for the first time
in their adult lives—raised expectations for leaders everywhere. The
implications of this development for definition of successful leadership have been profound.

As with any job, being chief executive officer of a major corporation had had its pluses and minuses. Among them—good pay. Salaries were—and remain—generous. Sandy Weill got $151 million for running Citigroup in 2000, Jack Welch $125 million for leading General Electric. Larry Ellison's pay as head of Oracle was $92 million.[1]

And high visibility. The faces of big-company chief executives grace the covers of magazines. Their speeches are widely reported; their pronouncements can move markets; they write books. You can't be a regular reader of the *Wall Street Journal* in 2001, for example, without knowing the names of, say, Michael Dell, Carly Fiorina, and Sir Richard Branson, never mind Welch or Bill Gates. Fame spans the globe. Thomas Middelhoff of Bertelsmann (Germany), Serge Tchuruk of Alcatel (France), and Li Ka-Shing of Hutchison Whampoa (Hong Kong) are nearly as well known outside their home countries as they are within.

However, there is no job security. Former Ford CEO Jac Nasser lasted about two years. Former Coca-Cola CEO Douglas Ivester lasted less than three. So did Lucent chief Richard McGinn. Remember Eckhard Pfeiffer of Compaq, Robert Allen of AT&T, and John Akers of IBM, all unceremoniously ushered out the door? They were long-lived as CEOs compared to G. Richard Thoman of Xerox (fired after less than two years) and Michael C. Hawley of Gillette (ditto). Lloyd Ward of Maytag Corp. resigned after fifteen months on the job. Mattel and Procter & Gamble also grace this list. "No, it isn't your imagination," said a report on this phenomenon. "CEOs really are getting the boot faster than they used to."[2]

In the old economy it was different. "The men who head the great corporations are unknown," wrote the famous economist John Kenneth Galbraith in his 1967 book *The New Industrial State*. "Not for a generation have people outside Detroit and the automobile industry known the name of the current head of General Motors."[3] Corporate leaders were well paid in Galbraith's day, but on nothing close to today's scales. And they tended to stay with the company a long time, until the board (routinely) approved a handpicked successor. Then again, why wouldn't CEOs of those days be unremarkable? The companies run by these men—they were all men—dominated their marketplaces. They were consistently profitable: "Among the largest corporations," wrote Galbraith, "the certainty of earnings is very great."[4] And so it didn't matter much who was at the helm, provided he was experienced and conservative.

And today? Competitive threats appear from every corner. Nothing else in the marketplace holds still, either. Production and communications technologies change from year to year, rather than from decade to decade. Distribution channels that once seemed as durable as Roman aqueducts dry up seemingly overnight. Consumers' tastes are mercurial; business customers no longer remain loyal to longtime suppliers. In this convulsive context, the man or woman at the top of a company faces challenges that would daunt Hercules. He or she must determine strategy; make the decisions that allow it to be executed effectively; communicate it to Wall Street, employees, the general public, and investors as well; ensure consistent growth of earnings while investing enough in innovations; inspire the troops—and manage all the other intangibles detailed in the next eleven chapters. No wonder it's hard to find men and women who can pull this off. No wonder, too, that boards of directors want to compensate generously the people in whom they place such outsized hopes.

Conclusion: The value of the intangible known as leadership has skyrocketed. In the Intangibles Economy, the issue of who runs a company *matters*.

A TALE OF TWO COMPANIES

In the extreme, the difference between a good CEO and a poor one can mean the difference between prosperity and the corporate poorhouse.

On the negative side of this ledger is Warnaco, the apparel group. When new CEO Linda Wachner took it public in 1991, its future appeared bright. It held licenses to big-name clothing lines, such as Calvin Klein and Ralph Lauren. There was money in the bank from the IPO. But over the next several years the company's prospects spiraled downward. Wachner embarked on an acquisition spree that ran up a debt of $3.1 billion, which eventually amounted to 30 percent more than the company's assets. She first ignored discounters such as Wal-Mart Stores, Inc., then offered them huge quantities of merchandise at fire-sale prices. She didn't cultivate critical alliances. Calvin Klein clothes were 40 percent of Warnaco's sales, but Klein himself became so disgruntled with her strategy that he sued both Warnaco and Wachner for cheapening his brand.

Behind the scenes it was worse. Wachner's style was variously described as imperious and bordering on the despotic. She became known for setting unrealistic goals and for laying into top executives when the goals weren't met. Turnover in the executive ranks was high; the company's Calvin Klein Kids unit, for example, went through five presidents in three years. In 2001 a retail consultant told *The Economist*, "She led this firm into the mud. Her conduct and miscalculations have been deplorable." Even so, Wachner managed to line her own pockets. In 1994 she was paid more than G.E.'s Welch. In 2000, the company registered a loss of $338 million, yet Wachner still took home about $3 million and continued to commute to work in Manhattan by helicopter. Her golden parachute was reportedly worth as much as $44 million, or four times what the company had in the bank when it filed for bankruptcy. That in effect made her (virtually) "unsackable"—Warnaco was thought to be unable to afford it.[5] However, by November 2001 she had "resigned" to the outspoken relief of Warnaco's shareholders.

While Warnaco was going down, another old-line company in an equally unglamorous industry was going straight up. In 1995 Sir John Browne took over the oil giant BP, then a struggling second-tier producer only recently recovered from a stretch of losses. Browne worked mostly behind the scenes for two years, then launched a series of dramatic moves that effectively catapulted BP into a leadership role in the oil industry. Among them are:

- He spent $48 billion in 1998 to acquire Amoco, then $27 billion to buy Atlantic-Richfield Corporation (ARCO). The moves ratcheted BP up into the number-three position in the industry; observers said it might soon move past Royal Dutch Shell into the number-two slot. The management team led by Browne also made BP into the largest U.S. producer of natural gas, nearing Browne's goal of 60 percent oil and 40 percent gas (versus 90–10 when he took over).
- He committed BP to massive involvement in so-called deepwater drilling, including extensive holdings in the Gulf of Mexico. Deepwater drilling is risky and expensive, but when it works it pays off handsomely, because per-barrel production costs can be cheaper than on land or in shallow water. BP hit pay dirt, turning up a sizable number of high-performing wells. Its production costs wound up lower than those of ExxonMobil or Shell, analysts said, and BP's growing expertise in deepwater rigs enabled the company to bring wells online faster than ever before. "The deep-sea plunge is the crucial element to achieving Browne's promise of turning in earnings growth of 10% a year even as revenue grows only half as fast," argued *Forbes* magazine.[6]
- Browne took positions on environmental matters that were nothing short of astonishing for the head of a major oil company. In 1997 he acknowledged in a speech that global warming may be worth paying attention to. (He was the first oil executive to do so.) He publicly committed BP to reducing its emissions of carbon dioxide by 10 percent

over 1990 levels by 2010.[7] He invested in cleaner forms of gasoline and diesel fuel, and in the development of solar and other alternative energy sources. (BP is the world's largest manufacturer of photovoltaic cells.)

Warnaco's stock reflected Wachner's moves, falling from $44 in July 1998 to $0.39 in June 2001 as the company entered bankruptcy. BP's stock price reflected Browne's moves. The stocks of major oil companies move pretty much in tandem, but from 1990 through 1994 BP's stock lagged well behind the others. From 1996 to 2001, oil stocks were all much more volatile, but BP was often in the number-one spot. In 2001 BP made *Fortune* magazine's list of Globally Admired Corporations. It ranked #5 on the magazine's 2001 list of highest-profit global companies.

BEYOND THE HEADLINES

Such stories are numerous in the Intangibles Economy. General Electric prospers mightily under Jack Welch, whereas Westinghouse, once a serious competitor, hires "five wrong CEOs in a row" and finally disintegrates.[8] We take it for granted that the leadership of a major corporation—the CEO and the team he or she develops—can provide an invisible advantage because it has a major impact on the company's performance and prospects.

But it isn't just a matter of anecdotal evidence; research bears out the point. In our Measures that Matter study, for example—reported in greater detail in chapter three, above—we assessed the importance of a variety of intangibles to the investment decisions made by Wall Street professionals. (Since the intangibles affect the market valuation of a company, we call them *value drivers*.) Two of the value drivers relating to leadership, Management Credibility and Management Experience, ranked among the top-ten nonfinancial metrics most utilized by these investors. Moreover, a change in Quality of Management was shown to have the largest overall effect on the percentage of P/E ratio increases for both the short and long-term for industries studied, including computing, pharmaceuticals, food, and oil and gas. Similarly, in the original studies that led to the creation of what we called the Value Creation Index (VCI), one set of intangibles was called Management Capability; it included indicators on CEO Reputation, *Fortune*'s management-quality score, *Industry Week*'s best-managed companies, and *Worth* magazine's Fifty Best CEOs mention. It is consistently ranked in the VCI as one of the top three drivers.

Other researchers have produced comparable findings. The communications consultancy Burson-Marsteller, for example, teamed up a couple of years ago with the research firm Wirthlin Worldwide to survey some 2,500 "stakeholders of business," including executives, financial analysts, and members of the business media. This team asked about the importance of the CEO to a company's reputation, what are a successful CEO's most important traits, and many similar questions. What they found was that a successful CEO is in many ways like a successful brand. "A favorable impression of a CEO enables people to personalize what seems impersonal, to put a face on the faceless and create meaning out of uncertainty," wrote Burson-Marsteller's Leslie Gaines-Ross and Chris Komisarjevsky. "A brand-name CEO can make a company stand out in a crowd." Reputation and recognition of this sort also translate into hard cash. Companies with the ten most-admired CEOs, said the researchers, "recovered almost four times faster from the stock-market correction on October 27, 1997, than did companies with the 10 least-admired CEOs." What's more, "a full 77 percent of our respondents reported being likely to buy stock based on the reputation of the CEO."[9] For a large-cap company, in short, a well-respected CEO can mean literally hundreds of millions of dollars in market valuation.

WHY DOES THE CEO MATTER SO MUCH?

A CEO is ultimately responsible for all the operations of a business: strategy, execution of strategy, earnings growth, market share, and other matters. But this has always been true. What's new in the Intangibles Economy is that the CEO is directly and primarily responsible for managing some other crucial intangibles. The four central tasks, in our view:

Creating the Vision

Call it "vision" or "mission" or simply (to use Leslie Gaines-Ross's term) "sense making." Whatever the term of art, it means articulating a picture of why the company is in business, why it matters, where it is going. In the past, no one would have attempted to create a vision for an *oil* company. And even today, Sir John Browne's positioning of BP can be (and has been) scorned by critics. But look at the effects. Suddenly BP is set apart from the pack. Suddenly, too, it is an attractive place for a bright young petroleum engineer to apply to, and an attractive repository for investment dollars. Morale builds. Browne told an interviewer in 1999 that he had asked BP employees how they felt about the environment. "They felt the following: They worry about global warming, their children talk to them about it, they think the company ought to get on the front foot about this." When he asked for suggestions about what the company might do, he was swamped with e-mails. "The number of responses was phenomenal. People believe that this is a principal value of this company: green."[10] The more the CEO tells the *story* of a company—what the company is all about—the more both the CEO and the company stand out in the minds of prospective employees, customers, and investors.

Developing the Management Team

A brand-name CEO attracts top talent. A CEO also sets the policies and procedures that determine whether people's talents will be cultivated, expanded, and encouraged. General Electric's leadership-development system is legendary, but not everybody realizes how directly the CEO has been involved in it. Welch himself reviewed the progress of key people, gave them written feedback, made sure they were on board with companywide intitiatives such as Six Sigma (and eased out those he thought were not). "We spend all our time on people," he says. "The day we screw up the people thing, this company is over."[11] The importance of this intangible lies in how it plays out over time. In the landmark study *Built to Last*, authors James C. Collins and Jerry I. Porras compared matched pairs of large companies—pairs in which one had consistently and thoroughly outstripped the other. Colgate-Palmolive fell behind rival Procter & Gamble, said the authors, in part because it neglected to develop bench strength in its managerial ranks. This was an area that P&G's leaders paid close attention to. "P&G's program for developing managers is so thoroughgoing and consistent that the company has talent stacked like cordwood—in every job and at every level," wrote one observer. P&G always expected to "have two or three people equally capable of assuming responsibility of the next step up," said another.[12]

Setting the Cultural Tone

A CEO generates the symbols that create and maintain a workplace culture. Southwest Airlines founder Herb Kelleher famously spent time slinging bags and working airport gates, sending the message that nobody's job is unimportant. IBM's Lou Gerstner showed up for work in a blue shirt, sending the message that the old "white-shirt" formality of IBM was coming to an end. Gerstner's work style—focusing on short, to-the-point communication, as opposed to the elaborate presentations for which IBM was so well known—was one tool that helped him effect the changes necessary to reshape Big Blue. By contrast, one of the factors that ended Rick Thoman's reign at Xerox was his inability to alter the staid, slow-moving, self-protective culture of the copier company. "I kept putting groups of people in rooms to work on fixing a problem, but it wouldn't get fixed because someone would disagree and the issue would not be settled," Thoman told a reporter.[13]

Planning for Succession

Which is longer, the list of large companies that have carried out a successful transition from one CEO to another—or the list of those that have found themselves in trouble after the transition? On the one hand we count so-far successful changeovers like those at Home Depot, Intel, American Express, Johnson & Johnson, Exxon, and Wal-Mart Stores. On the other hand we think of disasters that have happened at Enron, Xerox, Lucent, Compaq, Coca-Cola, Apple Computer, Rubbermaid, Mattel, and Toys "R" Us. Bizarre as it may sound, one of the most important jobs a CEO can do is prepare the way for a successful transition to the next administration. When it came time for Welch to retire from GE, the outgoing CEO spent a remarkable amount of his own time choosing his successor, Jeffrey Immelt.[14] But it surprised no one who had been following Welch's career and who understood his priorities. Way back in 1991, nearly a decade years before he actually announced his retirement, Welch said that from then on, choosing his successor was the most important decision he had to make. "It occupies a considerable amount of thought almost every day."[15]

CORPORATE GOVERNANCE

How does all this matter to anyone other than CEOs themselves—or the board committees charged with picking one? It matters for two reasons.

First, everybody in business—investors, competitors, suppliers, would-be employees—is constantly assessing the strength of companies. What are their prospects for the future? Can they withstand competitive assaults? Can they adapt to a changing marketplace? Our argument throughout this book is that any company's long-term strength depends mightily—sometimes primarily—on a dozen or so key intangibles. The quality of its leadership is among the most important in any such assessment. Companies that are capable of developing good leaders and putting them in place automatically enjoy a market premium. They seem stronger in the eyes of those around them. Companies that go through CEO after CEO, announcing that they have finally found the right person only to kick him or her out a year or two later, are destined to be the also-rans of the competitive race. When you evaluate a company, start at the top. Increasingly, while CEOs have less time to prove themselves, boards are criticized for the choices they make. Good corporate governance is an accepted measure of performance.

Second, what's true at the top is true throughout an organization: Leaders either lead or don't lead. Successful ones articulate a vision, develop people under them, create a culture in which people learn to work hard and cooperate, and plan for their own replacement. A CFO or regional vice president, a plant manager or brand manager—all are chief executives of their domains. And what they do matters greatly. In the famous Hawthorne experiments of the 1920s, researchers found that an employee's relationship with his or her supervisor was the key factor in determining job satisfaction, and subsequently, productivity. In a major study published a few years ago by the Gallup organization, researchers discovered much the same thing. Gallup's interviewers surveyed about a million workers, including 80,000 managers, over twenty-five years. They found that employee retention, productivity, and worker satisfaction vary greatly from one unit to another, even within the same company. The reason? "People may join a company because of its brand identity," said Gallup vice president Marcus Buckingham, "but how long they stay depends to a great extent on the quality of their manager."[16]

Leadership starts at the top. It doesn't end there.

STRATEGY EXECUTION 6

Intangibles such as R&D, proprietary know-how, in-
tellectual property and workforce skills, world-class
supply networks and brands are now the key drivers
of wealth production while physical and financial as-
sets are increasingly regarded as commodities.

—*Report on the Intangible Economy to*
the European Commission, October 2000

The story of Wal-Mart Stores is one of those sagas that you think you know, just because it has been repeated so often. Sam Walton starts a little store in Arkansas. He builds a few more. In expanding, he targets small towns and rural areas that are underserved by existing retailers. People in these markets aren't wealthy; quite the opposite. By tradition and by economic necessity, they'll buy only if the items in the stores are cheap. Hence the hallmark of Wal-Mart's strategy, then and now: *everyday low prices.*

But Wal-Mart didn't grow to be the world's largest retailer just on the basis of Sam Walton's good idea. Discount retailing is one of the toughest businesses around, and Wal-Mart has always had plenty of competition from chains that started out with better-known names and deeper pockets. What are its secrets?

In many respects Wal-Mart is just like any other discounter. It buys goods in huge volume, of course. It locates stores on the outskirts of town, where real estate is cheap. It keeps wages low, and it fights at-

73

tempts to unionize its employees. But to call Wal-Mart simply a discounter is like calling Tiger Woods just a golfer: It misses the point. Wal-Mart pushes costs down and keeps them there through a startling variety of sophisticated tactics that no competitor has ever knit together as successfully as Wal-Mart. Among them:

- Wal-Mart has never depended on any one vendor for more than 4 percent of its overall purchase volume. This gives the chain leverage over suppliers—leverage that it doesn't hesitate to use when suppliers try to raise prices. [1]
- Wal-Mart owns 3,000 trucks and 12,000 trailers, which are used to distribute inventory. Its competitors mostly use outsourced transportation. About 85 percent of its products are shipped through distribution centers; competitors use distribution centers for only 40 percent on average. These centers serve nearby Wal-Mart stores (150–200 per center) with the entire array of Wal-Mart products. All can be delivered all in a day's time. The cost savings in transportation alone is 2 to 3 percent over the competition. The system also ensures a near-100-percent in-stock position, and increases a store's selling space by reducing space required for storage. [2]
- Wal-Mart uses a satellite network to coordinate its ordering process. The network allows stores, distribution centers, and suppliers to share information so orders can be consolidated, thus minimizing excess orders and inefficient deliveries. At the same time, the network allows executives to know what is happening in specific regions, districts, stores, and departments—even with specific items. They can identify problems before they hit the sales floor and avoid unnecessary markdowns. [3]
- Internally, Wal-Mart utilizes an Internet application called "Pipeline" (developed with the help of Cisco Systems) that

links all of the company's employees and business partners to improve communication and productivity. Vendors can see how their products are selling and create "what-if" scenarios, then work with Wal-Mart on sell-through and pricing. Password protection provides varying levels of access to information. The site has an up-to-date telephone directory, plus information on insurance, company policies, and employee benefits. Users can log on and track their records, relevant messages, and earnings all online.[4]

- With 65 million transactions a week, Wal-Mart can save 18,000 hours a week just by shaving one second off every transaction! The company thus invested in a scanning system that covers four times as much area as any other scanner in the market. The system achieves the highest first-pass read rate by scanning top-down as well as left-to-right of the barcode.[5]

- Despite its low wages, Wal-Mart's turnover rate is low for the retail industry, which minimizes hiring and training costs. Promotions are based on performance rather than on seniority. Incentives include relatively generous stock options and bonuses. Despite occasional attempts at unionization, Wal-Mart Stores is doing something right in the workplace: It regularly makes the list of the 100 Best Companies to Work for in America (see chapter thirteen).

Take all these actions one by one and there's nothing too exceptional. Take them all together and the image is quite different, like a jigsaw-puzzle picture that suddenly is recognizable when all the pieces are in place. Wal-Mart has a strategy: everyday low prices. But Wal-Mart is able to *execute* its strategy thanks to all these tools and techniques. The company has identified what it needs to know and do in order to put Sam Walton's good idea into practice. It has developed a cluster of intangibles—essentially, the ability to manage the various tools and techniques—so that it can actually implement the idea. That ability, more than the strategy itself, is what differentiates Wal-Mart from its competitors.

The Importance of Execution

In some respects our study *Measures That Matter*, described in chapter three, only confirmed and put numbers on what people already knew. Intangibles are important. Traits like the quality of a company's leadership, its ability to innovate, and its brand equity have always mattered to professional investors, and all our research did was show how much these traits mattered. But sometimes research turns up a finding that nobody really expected. For us, the surprise was the intangible that wound up number one on the ranking. The most important non-financial driver of a company's value, in the eyes of our respondents, was a company's ability to execute its strategy. Not *quality* of strategy, note; that was farther down the list. Simply the company's ability to do what it says it is going to do.

The significance of strategy execution was an eye-opener. After all, books are written about strategy. Books are written about brand equity and human capital and other sets of intangibles. Nobody writes a book about what any competent businessperson is supposed to be able to do. The very word "executive"—ultimately derived from the Latin *exsequi*, essentially meaning to follow up on—means someone who *executes*.

So why is execution so important? Once again, it reflects the nature of the Intangibles Economy.

When the marketplace moved more slowly, strategies themselves mattered more than they do now. A good strategy took time to develop and more time to implement. Competitors might not even be aware of what a company was doing until a year or more into the game. Wal-Mart stayed under the radar of competitors, such as Sears, for years.

In today's marketplace the situation is different. Managers have been taught from the same case studies at similar schools. They have similar load sets on their computers. The same computers give them access to a dizzying array of information about companies, most of which isn't—and can't—be monitored by the companies themselves. The result: Sustainable competitive advantage is hard to come by. It's simply too difficult to protect your secrets, or even to develop a strategy that isn't obvious to your competitors. They know too much about your assets, your liabilities, your costs, your customers, your financial constraints. A budding Wal-Mart today would be written up all over, its business plan dissected and analyzed by investors and journalists and business-school professors. Managers in other companies would have read case studies of similar situations (so-called disruptive innovation) and would have ideas about how to respond.

The term *coevolution* describes a biological process in which species adapt to changes taking place in other species as they happen, and in some cases because they happen. So it is with business: Though more is known about what makes a successful business, business success is harder to achieve because the knowledge is is held by all, not just by a few. Competitors begin to devise strategies to counter yours as soon as they are aware of what you're doing. You have to adapt; they adapt to your adaptations, and so on. Investors' nomination of strategy execution as the number-one value driver may simply reflect how few managements are actually capable of carrying out their strategies in this fast, hypercompetitive, coevolving economy.

THE "EXECUTION" LENS

Strategy execution is like a lens that lets you peer into a company's operations. Ask why Wal-Mart or any other company is able to carry out its strategy so well, and you find yourself ticking off a variety of obvious and not-so-obvious elements. It is the fit, and the complementarity, among them, that makes the whole thing work. Strategy execution is also a lens into failure, or at least less-than-success. Three lessons from this intangible:

"Copycat" Strategies Work Only If You Can Execute Every Element

Consider the airline business in the United States. Even in the best of times it's a tough industry, capital intensive, and highly cyclical. (The terrorist attacks of September 11, 2001, made operational viability almost impossible to achieve.) Prior to September 11, among major U.S. carriers, only one—Southwest Airlines—had been able to grow steadily while earning regular profits. (Since then, Southwest has, again, outperformed its competitors.) This fact has not been lost on competitors, both existing and prospective. Start-ups have regularly modeled themselves on Southwest. Larger airlines such as United have created special low-fare units to compete with Southwest. Because Southwest's strategy has been widely written up and extensively studied, emulating it shouldn't be too hard. It buys only one type of aircraft, thereby minimizing training time and maintenance costs. It eliminates "frills" such as meals and movies. It flies mostly short-haul point-to-point routes, rather than the more common hub-and-spoke routing system. The airline also maintains a no-reserved-seat policy.

But Southwest is able to execute this strategy where others are not. One key to its success, for instance, is its 15 to 20 minute turnaround time, independent of security checks, about half what the rest of the industry requires to get planes unloaded, loaded, and back in the air. This more-efficient utilization of aircraft saves Southwest hundreds of millions of dollars in capital expenditures, thereby helping to keep costs low. It allows the airline to offer more flights, thereby helping it serve customers better. But fast turnaround is *hard*. It requires "superb coordination among several value-chain activities, including ticketing, catering, baggage handling, fueling, maintenance, weight and balance calculations, and flight plans and local clearances."[6] It won't work if gate employees drag their feet or do only what their job description calls for them to do. Southwest's employees don't. In an industry known for contentious labor relations, incidentally, the airline has never had a strike, even though its workforce is 82 percent unionized.

As for where all this devotion comes from, Southwest founder Herb Kelleher deliberately set about building what you could call a cult of the employee. Employees hear over and over that they are the secret to the airline's success. They are rewarded with bonuses and stock ownership; they are feted with regular parties. Kelleher knows this culture is one element that sets Southwest apart; at one point he told an interviewer:

> What keeps me awake at night are the intangibles. It's the intangibles that are the hardest thing for a competitor to imitate. You can get airplanes, you can get ticket counter space, you can get tugs, you can get baggage conveyors. But the spirit of Southwest is the most difficult thing to emulate. So my biggest concern is that somehow, through maladroitness, through inattention, through misunderstanding, we lose the esprit de corps, the culture, the spirit. If we ever do lose that, we will have lost our most valuable competitive asset.[7]

When a Company Runs into Trouble, the Answer May Be As Simple As Better Execution

Savvy CEOs who walk into a new company know that execution is often the first problem they must address. In a well-known incident, Lou Gerstner, when he was new to IBM, declined to offer a new vision for Big Blue; what the company needed, he said, was better execution. Robert Nardelli, the former GE executive who took over the reins of Home Depot in 2001, determined much the same thing.

The Home Depot has always tried to serve two segments of the market. Professional contractors come to the store purely for low prices and availability of stock; they don't need much in the way of advice or personal service from store personnel. Do-it-yourselfers, however, need all kinds of assistance. They rely on store personnel to help them plan a job, figure out what they need, choose between alternative tools or supplies, and find what they need in the store. In recent years the DIY segment has been growing, and Home Depot stores have had difficulty maintaining their reputation for friendly, knowledgeable service to the do-it-yourselfer. Among Nardelli's responses:

- The Home Depot launched a Web-based store network to service its customers from home. The online store offers 40,000 products at the same price as in the bricks-and-mortar stores. The network can be customized for do-it-yourselfers or professionals. It includes specialized payment plans and complimentary delivery options for bulk orders.[8]
- The Home Depot has invested in a customer-relationship management system to direct customer calls to a call center for speedier and more accurate response. The company is planning on employing as many as 1,000 agents in these call centers.[9]
- Nardelli has pushed for a Service Performance Improvement (SPI) initiative, hoping to reduce overcrowding in stores. Under the SPI, for instance, stores are not allowed to restock during business hours; rather, a night shift is added for restocking. Stores are also expected to step up their control over stray boxes and crates left in the aisles blocking traffic.[10]
- Though most Home Depot stores are set up in warehouse format, the chain is experimenting with new formats in new locations to fit the local shopper's taste. These include a so-called EXPO center design and a Villagers Hardware Store design.[11]
- The Home Depot has also contracted with marketing partners to take special-order telephone sales advertised through magazine ads to add efficiency and ensure service quality in customer orders. [12]

Whether Nardelli's efforts will succeed, of course, won't be known for a while. The economic decline and the events of September 11 have only made his task tougher. Like many intangibles, execution, too, plays out over time. Cisco Systems offers a cautionary tale on this score. The poster child for corporate success in the Internet era, Cisco registered annual growth rates in the 50 percent range, pulled off a series of successful acquisitions, and learned how to evaluate its financial position on a daily basis by developing an accounting "virtual close." It didn't hurt, either, that the company was led by an eminently quotable and photogenic CEO, John Chambers. In the fall of 2000, with Internet stocks beginning to tank, Chambers went so far as to announce that Cisco still expected to meet its forecasts of 30 percent to 50 percent growth for the foreseeable future. Execution appeared to be the name of Cisco's game.

Except it wasn't true. Less than a month and a half later, Cisco was forced to acknowledge that sales and profit growth weren't just slowing, they were turning south, and the company was going to have to lay off 17 percent of its employees. Chambers claimed, "We never built models to anticipate something of this magnitude."[13] However, subsequent investigation revealed that Cisco had had evidence of the looming sales decline, but overrode its own systems because the information being reported didn't square with its executives' view of the company's unlimited growth potential. The market's reaction was harsh and swift: Cisco's once-high-flying stock dropped 75 percent from its peak. The lesson here may be that strategy execution, at least in the market's eyes, is a double-edged sword. It lifts your stock when things are going well, but it can undercut you when the market perceives it has been misled about your ability to execute.

Execution Is the Key to Successful Mergers and Acquisitions

The Internet aside, what was the most fashionable growth strategy of the 1990s? Mergers and acquisitions. Companies in industries from health care to railroads decided that the best way to get bigger was to snap up competitors. Trouble was, virtually every serious study of mergers concluded that most failed to achieve the operational and financial goals used to justify the cost of the transaction. The market power that the new combination was supposed to create was elusive. The synergies designed to allow cost reduction were evanescent. In one such study, the consulting firm Booz-Allen & Hamilton examined seventy-eight deals valued at $1 billion or more, screened to represent different industry groups. One finding: Two years after the deal, "Fifty-three percent of the surveyed transactions had not met the expectations articulated at the time of the merger announcement."[14] The most frequently cited reason for the failure? Poor execution. "Mergers aren't for everyone," a vice president of the firm told the *Wall Street Journal*. "Sometimes CEOs bring the vision, but they don't bring the execution and tactical focus."[15]

The financial services sector was particularly plagued by this sort of underperformance in recent years. NationsBank's acquisition of Bank of America, for instance, led to a falling stock price, shrinking margins, and the departure of several key Bank of America executives, including CEO David Coulter. First Union's acquisition of CoreStates, BankOne's acquisition spree, and even Deutsche Bank's acquisition of Banker's Trust all had equally sorry outcomes. One might suppose on the face of things that these financial institutions have a more sophisticated understanding of the dynamics of merger and acquisition success. But all touted the potential synergies and cost savings without adequately exploring the effect the combinations might have on intangibles such as employee and customer loyalty. That analytical failure contributed to a significant loss of equity value.

What this tells us is that the complexity and intensity of the forces at play in the global economy conspire to make simply executing one's strategy the most challenging and potentially rewarding of today's management tasks. Challenging because globalization, technological developments, the rapid pace of change itself, and a host of other dramatic stresses contribute to the difficulties executives have in meeting their goals. Potentially rewarding because so few companies do it consistently and well so that those who do, stand out from the crowd. The violence to which the capital markets subject the securities of those who fail to meet their goals simply underscores the importance of doing so. To survive, organizations must execute well. To prevail means doing so better than your competitors.

COMMUNICATION
AND TRANSPARENCY

As intangible assets grow in size and scope more and more people are questioning whether their true value—and the drivers of that value—are being reflected in a timely manner in publicly available disclosure.

Arthur Levitt, Chairman (1993–2001),
U.S. Securities and Exchange Commission

In the past, companies tried to control the flow of information that reached the outside world. They talked only to a few favored analysts. They guarded company secrets. They changed course without much explanation. As organizations they were *opaque* rather than *transparent*. Plenty of companies would still like to operate in this manner, no doubt, but it's getting harder, maybe even impossible. As we saw in chapter three (and in the quote above from Arthur Levitt), there's a growing clamor for more and more disclosure of more and more kinds of information.

This is one bandwagon that businesspeople would be well advised to climb on, and the sooner the better. In the Intangibles Economy, we'll argue in this chapter, transparency provides (so to speak) an invisible advantage.

The Decline of the Analyst System

Sell-side analysts—those who follow particular industries and companies on behalf of brokerage houses—enjoyed an enviable position in the old economy, though not one without its difficulties. On the one hand they were cozy with the companies they covered. They got the earliest information. Their pronouncements were heeded by big investors and money managers; they could move share prices just by choosing one word rather than another; and they were nicely compensated, most of them earning well into six figures. On the other hand they had to walk a fine line. Analysts who issued too negative a report on a company might find that its executives no longer returned their calls. Worse, the same financial-services firms that employed the analysts were courting the companies they covered for investment-banking business. A "Chinese wall" was supposed to separate the two departments, but it could be hard for an analyst to remain objective in assessing a company when $20 million in underwriting fees might be at stake.

As it happened, this was a conflict that would soon spiral out of control. An early shot was fired as far back as October 1998, when a cover story in *BusinessWeek* announced: "The question for investors is, 'Can you trust your analyst?' Unfortunately the answer is not very much."[1] The Internet bubble brought things to a head. Analysts hyped Internet stocks relentlessly, and investors went along until the bubble burst. Then they—and the business press—began blaming analysts, precisely because of that conflict of interest. Morgan Stanley analyst Mary Meeker came to symbolize the problem. Her initial research reports on the Internet made her an authority on Internet-related companies. She assumed a high profile, issuing statements and making speeches. She began to be called in on deals. Companies gave Morgan Stanley investment-banking business precisely because she was there. Meeker never liked to speak ill of a company she covered, and she continued to rate Internet investments high long after the bubble had burst. "With rare exceptions," said an article on Meeker in May 2001, "she kept an outperform rating on all her stocks." At the time of the article, well after the collapse, she still had an outperform rating on Priceline (down to $4 from $162), Yahoo! ($19.50 from $237), and Amazon ($15 from $106).[2] By August, investors had begun filing lawsuits against Meeker and Morgan Stanley. Merrill Lynch had settled a similar lawsuit against analyst Henry Blodget for $400,000 earlier in the summer.[3]

As analysts fell from grace, regulatory bodies leaped into the fray. In May 2001 a subcommittee of the House of Representatives began hearings on how analysts conduct business. In June, the Securities Industry Association adopted a set of "best practices" guidelines aimed at increasing the independence of analysts and eliminating undue influence from investment-banking pressures. Later that month the SEC issued an "investor alert" warning individual investors against relying completely on analyst-research reports, and in July SEC chairwoman Laura Unger testified before Congress that some analysts had profited to the tune of hundreds of thousands of dollars by trading in the *opposite* direction from their public recommendations.[4] Around the same time, the National Association of Securities Dealers proposed rules mandating that analysts and brokerage houses disclose ownership in, or investment-banking business with, companies under coverage. Merrill Lynch issued a new policy prohibiting analysts from buying stock in the companies they cover. Merrill's competitors announced that they, too, were reviewing their policies. Meanwhile, Prudential Securities decided its best hope for competitive advantage was to drop investment banking—a field that it had never been particularly successful in—and focus on "unbiased" research. Soon after, Prudential's analysts were issuing "sell" ratings on 7 percent of the stocks they covered, as compared to less than 1 percent at other firms.[5]

The regulatory frenzy was only one factor working to undermine analysts. Another was so-called Regulation Fair Disclosure, or Reg FD, issued by the SEC in August 2000. According to Reg FD, companies could no longer provide information selectively to favored analysts; they were obliged to release all material data to everyone at the same time. "Say goodbye to analysts," wrote a *Wall Street Journal* columnist reflecting on the new rules in mid-2001. "The Securities and Exchange Commission Regulation Full Disclosure has already wiped out much of their value, and they're set for a beating at tomorrow's congressional hearing on conflict of interest."[6] Still another factor undermining the value of analysts, of course, was the Internet itself. With so much information on companies so widely and easily available, with data disseminated so quickly, the days of inside experts such as analysts were probably numbered anyway.

The Case for Transparency

The decline of the analyst is both cause and symptom of a more far-reaching phenomenon, namely that companies can no longer control the flow of information. It's just too hard. Many have tried to clam up in the wake of Reg FD, but information leaks out anyway. Employees send e-mails, or they change jobs and talk about their old employer. Customers and competitors gossip. Internet chat rooms light up with tidbits of information, speculation, rumors. Business journalists—some of them as knowledgeable as any Wall Street analyst—comb through SEC filings and report what they find or deduce. The market necessarily relies on any information it can get. In late 1999, Tyco International watched its stock plunge 50 percent in two months, just because an influential Dallas-based newsletter questioned its accounting practices. Tyco hadn't misstated its results, it turned out, but neither had it done a good job informing investors of why the numbers looked the way they did.[7]

But this is less a problem than it is an opportunity, a chance to manage your company's agenda in the public domain. Let's call it *communications and transparency capital*. The more information you provide (within reason), the more intelligent will be the response of those you hope will lend you money, invest in your equities, seek you out as a customer, or accept you as a supplier. Transparency attracts the customers, suppliers, and investors who are right for you and discourages those who are not. It increases the market's confidence in the quality of your strategy and your trustworthiness that you are able to execute it. In a market driven by smart, well-trained people with access to a myriad of information, it's wiser to ask them to make intelligent choices based on good information—the information you provide—than to assume you can hoodwink them, or cover up your weaknesses.

A case reported by Harvard Business School professor Amy Hutton—that of America Online—illustrates the power of just this sort of open communication.[8] And a case we worked on for Cap Gemini Ernst & Young shows what can happen when a company doesn't communicate well.

AOL

For starters, Hutton reminds us just how far AOL has come. In the early 1990s it was a struggling start-up, competing with the likes of CompuServe and Prodigy. Today, as AOL Time Warner, it's a globe-straddling media conglomerate. Second, consider how AOL Time Warner's business model has changed over that time. Originally, as AOL, it was a fee-based subscription service—an Internet service provider (ISP) pure and simple. When giant competitors such as Microsoft began muscling in on this territory, AOL began to court advertisers, and in turn began to look and act more like a media company.

Note how carefully and openly AOL Time Warner communicated all that to Wall Street. When it was an ISP, it treated marketing and software expenditures as capital investments, arguing that they would pay off over the life of a customer. When its strategy changed, it decided to expense these costs (as most media companies do), taking the requisite writeoff and lowering its reported earnings. Each time, AOL executives took their case to analysts and investors, carefully explaining how what they were doing reflected the company's strategy. "Honesty proved to be the best policy. . . . Analysts read [the change] as a signal that AOL's managers were anticipating the industry's evolution."

Finally, AOL went to great lengths to popularize and explain the nonfinancial metrics that drove their strategy. In the early days it reported the anticipated "member life" of its subscribers. Later it reported average daily use per member. In effect it set the agenda for a whole industry: "When AOL started reporting the number of users, for instance, analysts began asking its competitors how they fared on the same metric." It's important to note that AOL didn't stop reporting its financial metrics at that time, and whether one agrees or disagrees with the measures AOL used, the fact remains that they were innovative in trying to expand but not replace their traditional disclosures. These attempts added to investors' understanding of a new business and therefore to the company's luster.

Hutton's conclusion is worth quoting at length:

> *AOL's record is evidence that companies not only do not suffer from being open about their strategy but actually gain from it. Being cagey about a good strategy only makes the execution more expensive. Investors accord a higher rating to the stock of companies they understand, and for the companies involved, that translates into cheaper capital. Unlike in war, in business there is almost never any long-term benefit to concealing a strategy, and a competitive advantage that cannot be openly defended is unlikely to be sustainable. More often than not, companies that make it easy for analysts and investors to see where they are going come out ahead.*

Chemcorp

We saw the opposite situation firsthand a few years ago, when executives of a large European chemical company—call it Chemcorp—

asked us to help them understand the importance of intangibles to the value of their company and to discuss how the company could manage its intangibles better. We did what consultants do in a situation like this: We went out and gathered information. We conducted interviews with sell-side analysts and buy-side analysts. We conducted an internal analysis of the company's performance in the financial markets. Surprisingly, we found that while Chemcorp's wealth had grown faster than that of most of its competitors over the previous four years, the capital markets were expecting lower returns in the future.

What was behind this gloomy outlook? Just one set of factors: the low ratings that analysts gave Chemcorp's *nonfinancial* performance. Both sell-side and buy-side analysts placed Chemcorp near the bottom (compared to key competitors) on measures of strategic vision, shareholder orientation, and operational efficiency. The corporate culture was seen as sluggish and bureaucratic; new-product development was viewed as lagging; high ratings in other areas, such as quality of top management and strength in the marketplace, weren't enough to overcome the perceived negatives. In a particularly telling exercise, we compared the brand value of the company to its key competitors in the chemicals industry and found that the stock traded at a sizable discount. In fact, if certain competitors changed their names to Chemcorp *but kept their own financial data*, they would trade at 85 percent, 75 percent, and even 65 percent of their actual prices!

Needless to say, we recommended a comprehensive strategy for communicating as much as possible with the capital markets. We argued, too, that the company could not afford to continue to be so selective about the strategic, financial, product, process, and other information that it revealed. Reticence only raises the suspicion that there are major problems. Open, frank communication—communication that shows that the company understands the intangible drivers of value in its business—mitigates such suspicions and negates skepticism about its strategy.

WHAT SHOULD BE DISCLOSED?

"The world of business has become one giant talk show with conflicting opinions, presented minute by minute, impacting stock prices, consumer sales, government decision making, and finally corporate reputation," says Graham Phillips, former chairman of Young and Rubicam Advertising. "But just as skilled advertisers understand how to rise above the clutter of 30-second commercials, CEOs and their companies must be able to break through the avalanche of uninformed opinion, where rumors, half-truths, and sometimes incomplete media coverage dominate the day."[9]

How to do this? We believe the best approach is complete disclosure on two fronts.

Financial Indicators

The SEC in the United States mandates full disclosure of company-wide financials—That's already a step beyond some parts of the world. In Asia, the *Asia Wall Street Journal* reports that "key pieces of financial information in the region remain shrouded in mystery" and that investors and money managers are demanding more transparency.[10] Many non-U.S. companies are choosing to list shares on the New York Stock Exchange and NASDAQ despite being required to provide more information about their results and lines of business than they are accustomed to in their home markets. They understand our argument: The more forthcoming a company is about its financial results, the more likely investors will be to put their money into the company.

But if some communication is good, isn't more communication better? Why not communicate division and business-unit financials as well as consolidated ones? Why not get the more controversial information—stock option grants, for example—out of the footnotes and into the main text of a report? "Evidence is strong that corporations would benefit greatly if they threw open their books to the scrutiny of investors," wrote *Fortune's* Justin Fox a few years ago. Fox quotes Paul Miller, an accounting professor at the University of Colorado in Colorado Springs: "Fuller financial reporting," said Miller, "will attract investors who are looking for a management they can trust to perform consistently over the long run."[11]

In this context, Reg FD offers companies a chance to set their own financial agenda—showing investors what management thinks is important and demonstrating that they are not afraid to be judged by those standards. Already studies have found that the regulation is encouraging greater disclosure without (as had been feared) leading to greater volatility in stock prices.[12] To be sure, a management that discloses an agenda in effect holds itself accountable for carrying it out. But investors are already holding management accountable, and boards are booting out executives who don't do what they say they'll do. So the dangers of transparency may be illusory. The payoffs, however, are not.

Nonfinancial Indicators

Companies such as Shell, BP, Skandia, and others are already releasing data on a variety of intangibles, including internal measures, such as employee morale and external measures such as the impact of their operations on the environment. Shell UK's "Report to Society," for instance, assesses the company's performance on indicators such as customer confidence, discloses how the company is responding to social and environmental issues, and is audited for accuracy by Lloyd's Register Quality Assurance. The report also "attempts to make the company's organizational structures and management decision-making processes more transparent to those outside its boundaries," according to a study prepared for The Brookings Institution.

Which nonfinancial indicators should be disclosed? Whichever ones offer the keys to the company's performance, including its ability to attract capital. In general, the markets need to understand a company's strategy, as in the AOL case, and the metrics by which managers will gauge the strategy's success. From there on, key information will vary by industry: plant productivity, measures of quality or customer satisfaction, gauges of brand strength, plans for a CEO's succession, products in the R&D pipeline, and so on. If the customers for the information you provide believe that your reasons for focusing on those metrics are sensible and the methods used to gather them are sound, our research suggests that disclosure will redound to your benefit.

To be sure, the use of nonfinancial indicators got a black eye during the biotech boom of the early 1980s and the Internet boom of the past couple of years. In both cases the young companies that went public weren't making any money yet, and profitability was likely to be some years off. So investors—often with the companies' encouragement—began focusing on nonfinancial metrics. For the biotechs, it was drugs in the pipeline or alliances with established pharmaceutical companies. For the Internet startups it was catch-as-catch-can figures such as "hits" and the "stickiness" of their Web sites. These indicators were presumed to have a relationship to ultimate revenues and profitability, but that presumption turned out to be wrong. When companies share nonfinancial metrics, the burden is on them to show that these indicators matter—that they are connected in a real way to the company's future financial performance. That may be difficult, but then so is creating good advertising (to use Graham Phillips's analogy). Providing hard, demonstrably useful data is really the only way to break through the clutter of information in the marketplace. Companies that do so will find themselves rewarded by investors.

A LAST WORD

In the final analysis, openness is as much a matter of style and approach as it is of policy. Some companies seem to have it built into their DNA. The Mexican giant Cemex, held up as a model enterprise in several books about management, is well known for the quantity and quality of information it shares, both inside and outside the company. It is therefore seen as "one of the most investor-friendly companies in Latin America," as a Goldman Sachs analyst told *The Economist*.[13] AES, the fast-growing global power company headquartered near Washington, D.C., shares so much information with employees that it has had to declare them "insiders" in order to abide by SEC regulations. Its annual reports to shareholders are also unusually frank and self-critical. On the opposite side of the disclosure coin, Gillette has been known for years as particularly closed-mouthed. And AT&T went through a series of strategic redirections under CEO Michael Armstrong without communicating the reasons for the changes effectively to Wall Street.

Our research leads us to believe that returns to transparency, or full disclosure, exceed returns to secrecy. Knowing which intangibles drive your business and communicating that knowledge to the market create a form of capital that executives ignore at their peril.

BRAND EQUITY

*Postindustrial enterprises run on intangible assets,
such as information, research, development, brand
equity, capacity for innovation, and human resources.
Yet none of these intangible assets appear on a balance sheet. This is another way of saying that, according to today's accounting practices, the worth of
a brand name like Citibank or Ford has no value.*

—Walter Wriston,
former CEO, Citicorp

Three illustrations of the power of a brand, arguably the best-known
intangible:

VIRGIN

One criterion used to judge the value of a brand is what's known as
"brand length," or the extension of the brand into diverse markets. In
this category few brands have been as successful as Virgin Group PLC,
the company run by "celebrity" CEO Richard Branson. A glance at the
Virgin Web site shows a presence in markets ranging from air and rail
travel to mobile phones and financial services. "Branson contends his
biggest advantage is his all-embracing brand," read one report on the
company. "Virgin's red-and-white logo already adorns everything from
wedding dresses to vodka. His sprawling empire, which extends to

340 businesses and joint ventures, might look to some like a motley collection." Not Branson. "We're lucky to have a brand that works with almost any business," he says.[1] The company's latest pursuit? Branson hopes to turn virgin.com into an Internet powerhouse; his goal is to create one of the world's top ten portals. It's a crowded marketplace, but Virgin has a chance of success because of its powerful name. In early 2001 the site was attracting 1.9 million visitors a month.[2]

Branson is famous for stunts designed to promote Virgin's brand, particularly those signaling the opening of a new business. He drove a tank down Fifth Avenue in New York City to introduce Virgin Cola to the United States. He drove around London on a flatbed truck with twenty nude female models holding mobile phones (Virgin mobile phone service); rode a white elephant to India's parliament to persuade the government to allow Virgin Atlantic service in India (it worked); flew hot air balloons; and portrayed a drowning victim on Baywatch, all for the sake of publicizing the Virgin name. Says Branson, "Using yourself to get out and talk about it is a lot cheaper and more effective than a lot of advertising. In fact if you do it correctly, it can beat advertising hands down and save tens of millions of dollars."[3]

However, the fun and games have serious financial consequences. Listen to this account of Branson's entry into the Australian air market:

> *When Richard Branson announced plans for a low-cost Australian version of his high-flying Virgin Atlantic Airways last year, the news sent a chill through the local industry. It wasn't that Qantas Airways Ltd. and Ansett Australia, the titans of Australian air traffic, weren't expecting new competition; the same year, the federal government had formally relaxed industry ownership rules, for the first time allowing foreigners to own Australian carriers outright. But this was Richard Branson. The flamboyant Briton's reputation for inno-*

vation and aggressive marketing tactics set Australian in-
vestors to fretting that his discount-fare Virgin Blue would
provide stiff competition for Qantas and Ansett. Even though
Branson's new carrier was months away from its launch date,
investors hammered down Qantas' stock price by 20 percent—
a level from which it has never fully recovered. The Branson
buzz continued right up to a Virgin Blue launch party in July
that featured celebrities, dancing, and a photogenic, champagne-
spraying Sir Richard.[4]

Branson has shrewdly built up Virgin companies on the strength of its brand. For example, Virgin Bank was financed with $500 million from outside investors; Virgin retained 50-percent control without contributing any money. "We're launching new companies that are 100 percent funded by external investors based on the power of the brand," said Branson.[5] By some estimates, if Virgin Group were to be listed publicly, it would be worth around $8 billion.

LEXUS

In 1983, Toyota chairman Eiji Toyoda held a top-level meeting at which the company's leadership decided to create a new vehicle. The goal: to challenge the world's best luxury automobiles. In 1989, after extensive studies and testing, Toyota introduced the Lexus. The car was priced 40 percent below Mercedes-Benz and 10 to 20 percent above Lincoln and Cadillac. Its impact on the market was immediate and strong. The Lexus LS 400 was named Best Imported Car of the Year by the Motoring Press Association just five months after its introduction. In 1990 it was ranked the number-one car line in J. D. Power and Associates' Initial Quality Study. Since then, Lexus has garnered nearly every excellence award in the auto industry multiple times, and has built a brand name synonymous with superior quality, performance, and customer satisfaction. In 1999—just a decade after it was launched—Lexus surpassed Mercedes as the top-selling luxury brand. In 2000 it was honored as the number-one Nameplate in Long-Term Dependability (J. D. Power and Associates) for the sixth time in as many years of eligibility, and the number-one Nameplate in Customer Satisfaction (also J. D. Power) for the ninth time in ten years.

It's not surprising that Lexus cars are of high quality, since parent company Toyota has a reputation for near-flawless manufacturing. But the real secret to long-term dependability is post-sale service. Lexus's parts and service managers complete multiyear training programs in automotive studies; in several countries they were the first managers in the industry to be professionally certified in automotive management. Lexus conducts ongoing employee training sessions in areas such as customer satisfaction, customer focus groups, service-advisor technical and administrative training, technician training, and certification up to "Master" level. Lexus also provides extensive support for technicians, such as an online connection to centers in the United States and Japan to assist difficult diagnoses.

In 2000 and the first half of 2001—scarcely more than a decade after the car's inroduction—Lexus was the best-selling luxury car in the United States; in mid-2001 it had experienced thirteen consecutive months of record sales. Remarkably, Toyota was not resting on its laurels. Worried that the Lexus brand was insufficiently defined in the minds of consumers, the company was seeking a consultant to help it map out its brand strategy for the future. "We want to keep this momentum going," said vice president of marketing Mike Wells. "We want to clearly identify that Lexus magic."[6]

THE U.S. MARINE CORPS

Walk into a marine-recruiting office—the one in Brockton, Massachusetts, say—and you don't find a drab, government-issue office like those that serve the army, navy, and air force. Instead you see what looks like a miniature version of a marine outpost. On the ceiling is fishnet, designed to replicate a jungle, with vines growing across it. On the walls are American flags, awards, sabers, swords, rifles, GI Joe marine dolls, military books, Semper Fi stickers, uniforms, medals, model and authentic guns, bullets, bombs, and targets. Over in the corner is a video setup where prospective recruits can watch promotional films. The movies are loud. The martial music makes you stand up a little straighter, and the nerves at the back of your neck tingle. They show smart, high-energy young people marching, operating heavy machinery, or coming home from boot camp, their friends and family members both proud and awestruck by their bearing and accomplishment.

The Marine Corps offers benefits such as college tuition, but the benefits aren't emphasized in the recruiting process. The Corps wants recruits to want to be marines for the sake of being marines. They define "marine" with three characteristics: smart, tough, and elite. Advertisements show a chess game or maze (to emphasize intelligence), drop comments such as "pain is just weakness leaving the body" (toughness), and coin slogans such as "The Few. The Proud. The Marines" (elite status). The recruitment process itself is intense (though it is only a harbinger of the intensity of boot camp). It's peppered with questions such as "When are we going to make you a Marine?" and teasers such as "Maybe you can be one of us." Recruits choose from eleven so-called benefit tags, listing the characteristics or objectives (such as Belonging, Strength, and Courage) they might hope to gain from being a marine. Recruiters focus on these, and hammer home the idea that joining the marines will change recruits' lives. In boot camp, the definition of what it is to be a marine is reinforced at every turn. ("The purpose of boot camp," said one marine, is to "instill the discipline which will cause that marine to stand and fight when every inborn instinct tells him to run.") At graduation, the successful candidate receives an Eagle, Globe, and Anchor (EGA), a uniform pin worn on the collar or hat, and is declared a marine "always and forever." In turn, individual Marines are legendary not only for their fighting prowess but for their devotion to the Corps and its ideals. And the service enjoys the highest esteem among the general public of any of the armed forces.

Marine recruiters, of course, are something like salespeople—but they're motivated not by commissions but by intangibles. Colonel Tom Tyrrell, commanding officer of the First Marine Corps district (which oversees the northeastern United States, including the Brockton office) gives awards to successful recruiters, ranging from his personal cell phone to "the shirt off his back." It's the rank itself that is revered here, and acknowledgment from someone with this rank is what's important. As with the "coins" passed out to soldiers by army, navy, and air force officers in recognition of special contributions or efforts, the reward's value lies not in monetary worth but in the fact that it comes from a commanding officer. In effect, such tokens are the ultimate intangible reward.

Brands in the Intangibles Economy

Volumes have been written on the management of brands such as these; we don't want to repeat it all here. What's interesting from our perspective is the relationship of *brand*, with all its various meanings, to the Intangibles Economy.

The Value of a Brand in Today's Marketplace Is Huge, and Probably Growing

Yes, it's tough to measure exactly what a brand is worth. But various methodologies have been constructed to assess the value a company can derive from a well-known brand. The Young & Rubicam BrandAsset® Valuator is based on interviews with more than 90,000 consumers in thirty countries; it correlates brand strength with the financial performance of the brand's owner, and shows that well-managed brands yield higher margins, more profit, more growth, and lower risk.[7] Interbrand, a U.K.-based research and consulting firm, judges brands by projecting the net earnings of branded products and then, through interviews, assessing what proportion of those earnings can fairly be attributed to the brand itself. By this methodology a brand such as Coca-Cola (number one on Interbrand's 2001 list of the world's most valuable brands) is worth nearly $70 billion. The value of the Apple Computer brand (number forty-nine) is about $5.5 billion, or roughly 80 percent of Apple's market capitalization at the time.[8]

The growing value of a brand can be seen in how widespread the practice of branding has become. Business-to-business marketers such as IBM are as likely to spend money on brand awareness as consumer-goods manufacturers. So are financial-services firms (think of Merrill Lynch and Charles Schwab), individuals (Martha Stewart), even places (I ♥ NY and its many emulators). The growing importance of brands reflects the range of choices available to customers today, and the ease with which they can learn about alternatives. "That's why companies that once measured their worth strictly in terms of tangibles such as factories, inventory, and cash, have realized that a vibrant brand, with its implicit promise of quality, is an equally important asset."[9]

The Power of a Brand Comes from the Customer's Experience—an Intangible—Not Just from Dollars Spent on Marketing

Sound obvious? It wasn't to the dot-coms, which poured millions of dollars into advertising and marketing without noticeable result. For many, their first goal after raising capital was to "create a brand." But their advertising had little effect. A U.K. survey, for example, found that Internet portal Lycos had spent £11.5 million on advertising, yet 68 percent of adults had never heard of Lycos while only 11 percent claimed to be familiar with the brand. Online bank First-e spent £6.5 million, but 89 percent of adults were unaware of the brand. The research firm, brand consultancy Headmint, concluded that the consumers surveyed "had little or no sense of what these companies are trying to offer, let alone a relationship with the brand."[10] It was no different in the United States. In Super Bowl XXXIV (2000), seventeen of the thirty-six companies buying the super-expensive TV time slots ($2.2 million for thirty seconds) were dot-coms. As of the writing of this book (in mid-2001)—just a year and a half later—seven of those seventeen had gone out of business. Computer.com spent $3 million of its $5.8 million in first-round venture financing on Super Bowl ads. It has since been sold.

Regis McKenna of the McKenna Group, perhaps the dean of high-tech marketers, told a recent conference that too many start-ups "think that the brand comes before the experience." On the contrary, he said: a company first needs to determine what its value proposition or "promise" to customers is, and to be able to deliver it. "The last thing you want is awareness when you haven't yet figured out what your promise is. So wait on awareness, and work hard on the promise."[11] One (current) Internet company that has followed this advice is BlueNile.com, which sells diamond jewelry. The company targets first-time diamond buyers, mostly male. It assuages their anxiety about buying diamonds (let alone over the Internet!) by providing tight online security, a step-by-step guide to diamond buying, an expert sales staff (with a call-in option), next-day delivery, a ten-day examination period, and a thirty-day return privilege, no questions asked. New clients come mostly from word of mouth rather than from advertising, so if the company can't deliver on its promise, it will fail. So far it is on track: Sales in 2000 were close to $50 million, about half the level needed for profitability, and in 2001 the company secured a $15-million credit line from GE Capital to build inventory and continue its growth.[12]

Successful Brands Depend on Astute Management of Other Intangibles

Richard Branson is a savvy brand builder and deal maker. But one root of his company's success is his idea that employees come first, before customers and certainly before other stakeholders. If you treat your employees well, runs the theory, they will be happier—and in turn will make your customers happier. Branson tries to meet as many employees as possible. He attends orientations, takes entire flight crews out to dinner, takes notes of their conversations, and responds to suggestions and complaints. He also responds personally to all letters he gets from employees. Then, too, Branson has been known to give major rewards to top performers. A couple of years ago he brought twenty employees with him to vacation on his Caribbean island, including a switchboard operator, a pilot, a housekeeper, and a reservations clerk. He throws an annual summer party for all Virgin employees at his country home, which lasts seven days; more than 25,000 employees attend each year. In return, "working for Virgin, especially in Britain, is nothing short of a badge of honor."[13]

Most companies can't suddenly turn themselves into a Virgin. But management of other intangibles can contribute to any company's brand. Mobil's "SpeedPass"—an innovative technology that is so far unique—instantly differentiates the company from other purveyors of gasoline and roadside convenience items. Starbucks invests in employee benefits to build morale and encourage long-term employment, because it knows a surly employee would undermine the brand. "If we want to exceed the trust of our customers, then we first have to build trust with our people," company chairman Howard Schultz told a reporter. "Brand has to start with the culture and naturally extend to the customers."[14]

Or take the phenomenon known as "cause marketing." According to a 1999 study conducted by Cone Inc., a marketing consultancy, and Roper Starch Worldwide, a research firm, Americans look positively on companies that support social causes such as charities or research efforts on diseases such as breast cancer. Two-thirds of respondents say they have greater trust in companies that are aligned with a social issue. Two-thirds also say they would be likely to switch brands to a supplier associated with a good cause, other things being equal. Nine in ten workers in companies with a cause program "feel proud of their companies' values versus 56 percent of those whose employers are not committed to a cause."[15] Of course, the "cause" doesn't need to be external to the company. Ice-cream maker Ben and Jerry's, cosmetics retailer The Body Shop, and oil giant BP all, in different ways, trade on a professed commitment to protecting or enhancing the natural environment.

Successful Brands Sell Intangibles (As Well As Tangibles)

The Marine Corps is "selling" young people the hope of acquiring desirable personal characteristics, of belonging to a group that is unique, and of serving their country. The power of these intangibles is substantial; after all, the Corps is asking these same prospects to submit themselves to substantial personal hardship for little money and possibly even to risk their lives. In the commercial world, the Virgin brand stands for a quite different set of attributes, but may be only a little less powerful. It seems to represent David vs. Goliath (Virgin competes against British Airways, EMI Music, and Coca-Cola, among other big corporations). It is associated with better deals, better service, fantastic customer loyalty, and more fun. "It's a brand-builder's nirvana, made all the more impressive because the brand is all that ties together (the) disparate Virgin businesses."[16]

Intangibles matter even when the product itself is quite tangible. The buyer of a Lexus is acquiring a well-engineered, comfortable luxury automobile, complete with good service. But he or she is also buying a status symbol; the Lexus presumably advertises both the buyer's financial situation and his or her good taste—membership in an exclusive club. This is a tricky value proposition to establish and maintain. Nissan's Infiniti model, launched at the same time as the Lexus, stumbled badly. One of its first two vehicles, the M30, was characterized as bland and borrowed, little more than an enhanced Nissan Maxima. Its initial advertising campaign was widely ridiculed. (Who wants to be the proud buyer of a status symbol whose marketing campaign is the butt of jokes?) Though the car has been improved, the brand has never matched Lexus. Cadillac, meanwhile, was the victim of its own success. Sales boomed during the late 1970s, peaking at more than 350,000 in 1978. But the glut of Cadillacs on the road led to a loss of distinctive brand identity, and sales subsequently nosedived. Hoping to avoid just such a fate, Lexus is limiting the number of cars each of its dealers is allowed to sell. "A luxury brand can't push volume, otherwise you don't have any focus at all," says Jim Hossack, who covers the market segment for Auto-Pacific. "Short-term, you and your dealers all go to the bank, but long-term it's the wrong thing to do."[17]

Finally, Brand Interacts Dynamically with Financial Performance

It affects the numbers and is in turn affected by them. In our Measures That Matter study, we learned that nonfinancial data have an indirect impact on other nonfinancial criteria, in areas in which the investor has little or no information. For instance, if investors like the product development effort of a pharmaceutical company, they tend to judge the company's overall performance more favorably than they would otherwise. They will also perceive criteria such as the company's brand image, or perhaps even customer satisfaction, better—again, even in the absence of any information on these factors. A one-point improvement in management quality, for example, may also yield a lift in brand power. These incremental changes in performance have long-term as well as short-term influences, *if* the company can sustain the improvement.

This "brand halo" effect has been the subject of extensive discussion in academic literature. It is closely related to both nonfinancial and financial performance. What this suggests is that *all nonfinancial criteria are fed by performance, and, in turn, feed the perception of performance.* And if a firm does not strategically manage key nonfinancial measures, its operating performance and the value of its shares will suffer.

REPUTATION

*Corporate reputation is a company's most enduring
and lasting asset.*

—Leslie Gaines-Ross,
Chief Knowledge Officer, Burson-Marsteller

In a sense a company's reputation is the ultimate intangible. It's literally nothing more than how the organization is perceived by a variety of people. It is slippery, volatile, easily compromised, impossible to control, amorphous. It is also all-too-widely ignored by corporate executives, who are prone to throw up their hands in despair at something so difficult to grasp. But reputation isn't so different from the other intangibles. Like them, it is subject to definition, analysis, and management. And the payoff from systematically managing a company's reputation can be enormous.

HOW IS REPUTATION DEFINED?

Since reputation is a matter of perception, researchers usually attempt to quantify it through surveys. What companies do you most admire? How would you rank them on the following criteria?

Not surprisingly, methodologies differ. *Fortune*, which conducts the granddaddy of reputation surveys for its annual "Most Admired Companies" feature, surveys business executives and sell-side analysts. The *Financial Times* limits its own survey—for its "World's Most

Respected Companies" list—to chief executives. Harris Interactive and the New York City–based Reputation Institute annually interview a sample of the general public. (The results are published in the *Wall Street Journal*.) Other researchers—Burson Marsteller, Corporate Branding LLC, and others—use their own approaches. Survey questions differ as well. Where *Fortune* focuses on eight attributes, the Reputation Institute uses twenty. Reputation Institute Executive Director (and New York University professor) Charles Fombrun charges that both the magazine and the *Financial Times* wind up giving too much weight to financial indicators, precisely because they limit their surveys to businesspeople. Ask employees and consumers, he says, and you'll get "quite different points of view on whom they regard highly."[1]

Yet it's easy to overrate the differences. For one thing, some companies show up on nearly everybody's list—General Electric and Wal-Mart are two examples—and there's invariably a good deal of overlap. This suggests that reputation, however quantified, exists independent of the precise measuring tool. For another, the particular kind of reputation that a company seeks to manage depends in good measure on the nature of its business. Sears or Disney may be more interested in its reputation among the general public than a company that sells primarily to business customers. Finally, no company's reputation exists in a vacuum. A couple of years ago, Lucent Technologies made *Fortune*'s list, while Xerox made the Reputation Institute's. It's a safe bet that neither company will be on anybody's list unless and until it gets back on its financial feet.

Reputation is not the same as brand, though the two intangibles are obviously related. *Brand* refers to the cluster of attributes and emotions customers associate with a particular product or set of products, including those products' value and functionality. *Reputation* refers to what a variety of stakeholders—not just customers but suppliers, other businesses, investors, employees, regulators, and the community at large—think of a whole company. While the *Exxon Valdez* disaster didn't change anybody's opinion of the quality of Exxon Corp.'s products, it certainly affected many, many people's perceptions of the company as a whole.

WHY IT MATTERS

However it's defined, reputation matters precisely because we live in an Intangibles Economy. *Employees* have a choice of where they work, even in a downturn (as recent experience has shown). If a company's value resides largely in the talent it attracts and in the intellectual property these employees generate, then the ability to attract the best people is priceless. *Investors* have a choice as well. A company's ability to attract capital depends on its reputation as well as on its financial results—in part because reputation seems to correlate with long-term financial performance. In our Measures That Matter study, several indicators related to reputation, including customer perception and environmental and social policies, ranked among the intangibles valued by the Wall Street professionals we surveyed.

Customers in particular like to do business with companies they respect, and shun companies that they don't. According to the Millennium Poll on Social Responsibility, close to 50 percent of American consumers say they "reward or punish companies' actions by buying or not buying their products or speaking out against the company."[2] A survey conducted for the Reputation Institute found that nearly a quarter of consumers had boycotted a company during the previous twelve months simply because they didn't agree with its policies or actions. "I would get a tow truck before I used Exxon or Mobil gas," a fifty-one-year-old woman told the *Wall Street Journal* in 2001. "I used Mobil all the time before the merger, but I believe I must take a stand over that horrible, disgraceful Alaskan oil spill by not giving Mobil or Exxon another cent."[3] The spill, it should be remembered, occurred more than a decade earlier.

Any large company, moreover, runs the risk of experiencing a major catastrophe. A product is found—or believed—to be flawed

(Firestone tires, Intel chips). A product makes somebody sick (Coke) or pollutes the environment (Exxon). A company has a horrendous accident (Union Carbide) or runs afoul of the law (Archer Daniels Midland). Such events typically have devastating short-term consequences on a company's stock price. Intel lost $3 billion in market cap after a minor flaw was discovered in one of its chips. Texaco lost more than $1 billion after allegations surfaced of racial discrimination in the executive suites. The event in question need be no more than unproved allegations. In 1995, Motorola lost about $6 billion in market cap after the first stories appeared linking cell phone use with cancer.[4]

How a company handles such a catastrophe goes far toward determining how great the repercussions will be. But so does the company's prior reputation. In the Tylenol scare some years back, as is well known, Johnson & Johnson followed a model strategy, immediately acknowledging the seriousness of the situation and taking fast, costly steps to get Tylenol off the shelves. Perrier took its water off the market when it discovered possible contamination in the source; McDonald's UK stopped selling British beef in the wake of the mad-cow disease scare. The three companies drew on and enhanced their reputation in so doing. Intel, in the flawed-chip fiasco, was more or less a model of what not to do, first denying that the flaw existed and then denying its importance. Still, Intel was able to recover relatively quickly because of its prior reputation. Exxon's reputation, by contrast, still lags, even though the company has long since recovered financially.

As with so many aspects of business, the Internet has added a new urgency to the management of reputation. Information—true or false—is spread instantly, all over the globe. Anticorporate sites, such as walmartsucks.com, have proliferated, and serve as repositories for grievances of all sorts, real and imagined. Warren Buffett once said that it takes twenty years to build up a reputation and five minutes to ruin it; in the age of the Internet that's no longer hyperbole.

Research suggests that more and more businesspeople are coming to understand the importance of reputation. In a poll of nearly 600 CEOs conducted by *Chief Executive* magazine and the Hill and Knowlton Corporate Reputation Watch, 94 percent of respondents agreed that reputation was "very important" in the realization of a company's strategic objectives, and 37 percent reported that they were formally measuring their companies' reputations.[5] All of which begs the question: Have corporate executives learned to manage this intangible? Doing so effectively creates an invisible advantage—while failing to do so can create a highly visible *dis*advantage.

Managing Reputation: Monsanto

Back in 1979, the chemical giant Monsanto was taking a hard look at its business. Then-CEO Jack Hanley was worried about continuing to focus on chemicals. It was a commodity business. Regulatory pressures were mounting. The industry was viewed poorly by environmentalists, and Monsanto's stock price was languishing. So Hanley launched a foray into agricultural biotech, pouring hundreds of millions of dollars into research and development. The "new" Monsanto story would impress Wall Street, executives believed. It could also do some good in the world. Monsanto was hopeful that the genetically engineered crops it was beginning to develop would prove just as fruitful as the Green Revolution of the 1950s and 60s: These crops would provide more food and better food for more people.

Jump-cut to 2001. In Italy, 120 tons of Monsanto corn (maize) suspected of containing genetically engineered materials not approved by the European Union are seized in a police raid. In Brazil, a mob of more than a thousand protesters breaks into one of Monsanto's experimental farms and proceeds to yank genetically modified (GM) corn and soybean crops out of the ground. Though less aggressive, the anti-GM wave begins to appear in the United States as well. Protesters picket not only Monsanto's headquarters in St. Louis, but also some of the company's larger customers. At Starbucks Corp.'s annual meeting, picketers rally against the use of GM soy and corn products (as well as milk produced with bovine-growth hormones). McDonald's and several other large fast-food chains announce that they will no longer use Monsanto's GM potatoes. Kellogg's phases out the use of GM products in Europe—not for safety reasons, "just to please customers," the company states.[6] Meanwhile, U.S. farmers cut back on the number of GM seeds they plant, fearing loss of international sales.

What happened? Ironically, Monsanto had done most of what it set out to do. The nearly $10 billion company had become a leader in the production of genetically modified seeds. Those most familiar with Monsanto's products—farmers—are big fans of the GM products, which improve the production of major crops. Scientists have told the U.S. Food and Drug Administration that genetically modified foods offer definite health benefits by delivering more nutrients, reducing spoilage, and lowering chemical contamination. Monsanto's net sales reached $5.5 billion in 2000. It has been praised for its workplace culture and for being a leader in the introduction of new products and business processes. On the negative side, it was criticized even by its friends for poor public relations and overaggressive marketing, particularly overseas—pushing new biotechnology products into areas too rapidly or without giving people the freedom to evaluate the new technology.[7]

At any rate, neither its successes nor its failures meant much in the face of the protest. Dubbing Monsanto's products "Frankenfoods," green activists pummeled the company's reputation, and with it the stock price. In June 1998, Monsanto was meeting Wall Street's financial expectations—revenues up 28 percent, earnings up 5 percent—yet its stock hit a new 52-week low, losing 35 percent of its value in a year. (The stock market as a whole was then in the midst of the 1990s bull market; the S&P 500 was up 30 percent for the same twelve months.) "The valuations are based on perceptions—not reality," said agribusiness analyst Sano Shimoda. "But in this case, perception—consumer confidence—has become reality."[8] When Monsanto's subsequent attempt to merge with American Home Products failed, then-CEO Robert Shapiro must have thought things couldn't get any worse. They did. Shapiro gave a keynote address on genetic engineering at the State of the World Forum in San Francisco later that year. He was hit in the face with a tofu creme pie, courtesy of Frankenfoods protesters.

Monsanto finally merged with Pharmacia & Upjohn in April 2000, renaming the combined entity Pharmacia. In October 2000, Pharmacia decided to spin off a new Monsanto, consisting of only the agriculture business, in a partial IPO. This time, the company had apparently learned its lesson about the importance of managing reputation and customer perception. "Monsanto is determined to ride out the GM backlash," said a Reuters report, "and has adopted a new low-key approach heavy on education and outreach, and light on the aggressive promotional moves of years past."[9] The new company comes complete with "The New Monsanto Pledge," a declaration outlining five key elements including dialogue, transparency, respect, sharing, and delivering benefits. (The original "Monsanto Pledge" was made in 1990 as a statement of environmental responsibility.) In line with its first key element—dialogue—in June 2001 the company formed a wheat industry advisory committee composed of a cross-section of industry experts to counsel Monsanto on the role of biotechnology products in wheat.

Monsanto's new approach to managing its reputation has likely contributed to the steady growth of its stock price since the recent IPO. In contrast with past stock performance, even though the company's revenues and earnings have been down, the stock went from under $20 per share in October 2000 to nearly $32 per share by November 2001. No doubt protests and lawsuits will follow the company wherever it goes, and transforming its image will forever be a challenge give the nature of its business. Yet although Monsanto may never be on the good side of all environmentalists, at least it is trying to show that it is a company that is concerned and wants to understand all implications, both positive and negative, of genetic engineering. "Carrying out the biotechnology acceptance strategy longer term," says spokeswoman Lori Fisher, "that would be key to our company's future."[10]

MANAGING REPUTATION: LESSONS

What can a company do to manage its reputation? It's rarely a matter of simply taking out more corporate "image" ads (though a strong, consistent image advertising campaign can certainly help). We recommend a five-step process:

1. Take stock. What is your company's reputation now? Is it "most admired"—or is it at the opposite end of the list? If your company isn't included on somebody's U.S. or global list, there are research firms who will sell you information on where you stand in your industry. You may need to do some research of your own, but it'll be worth it. Monitor your reputation on the Internet as well. In the Chief Executive/Hill and Knowlton survey, only 11 percent of CEOs said that their companies kept a regular eye on their online reputations, even though they knew it was important to do so. "A disconnect between awareness and action," said a report on the survey.[11]

Assessing your company's reputation, of course, means knowing what you're measuring. What are the values that you would like to stand behind your company's reputation? Reputations aren't created from nothing; they reflect real principles and priorities. Sometimes the values that stand behind a reputation are intrinsic to the company's business—Wal-Mart's everyday low prices, Merck's commitment to human health. In other cases the values reflect internal or external commitments: a "great place to work" workplace, a commitment to the environment, a commitment to a cause or charity. Ronald McDonald is as important a part of McDonald's corporate reputation as its hamburgers, maybe more.

2. Count. Equally important, what are the metrics that are most appropriate for tracking progress or deterioration in reputation? Customer surveys are surely useful, but so are indices such as published reports in the media or in the investment community. The British telecommunications provider NTL tracks the number of people who apply for jobs through the company's Web site. "We see that as a testament to the strength of our reputation," says the company's group marketing director.[12] Interestingly, the companies that enjoy the best reputations also tend to use all sorts of measurement in comparison to other companies. The Hay Group conducted a survey of the "Global Most Admired" companies on the 2000 *Fortune* list and found significant differences on this score between these companies and their less-admired counterparts. The Most Admired are more likely to chart customer-relations indicators such as satisfaction and loyalty. They are more likely to track retention and career development. "In contrast with those of their peer companies, senior executives of the Most Admired Companies believe that many of these performance measures encourage cooperation and collaboration. Many executives reported that such measures help their companies to focus on growth, operational excellence, customer loyalty, human-capital development, and other critical issues"—all issues, it might be added, that affect a company's reputation.[13]

3. Take charge. Who is responsible for cultivating your company's reputation? Chances are, nobody is—or that this is just one among many responsibilities supposedly shouldered by the CEO. Reputation cuts across divisions, departments, brands, and locations, and it affects them all. The corporate communications department can help you get a message out, but it shouldn't be in charge of determining what the message is to be. That is ultimately the province of the CEO, but he or she will need help from a variety of senior managers. Some companies, such as investment bank UBS Warburg, have hired reputation managers.[14] At Monsanto, reputation became so important that it engaged the entire executive team.

4. Take action. Reputations are made, not born. They are the result of deliberate choices. A reputation for sterling customer service, such as Nordstrom's or L.L. Bean's, comes about because the company is willing to invest large amounts of money in staff training, refunds for returns, and so on. A reputation for quality manufacturing such as Toyota's is built by years of dedication to process improvement. At the same time, small, specific decisions can make a big difference. Remember Paul O'Neill's commitment to safety when he took over Alcoa (pages 56–57). This was a commitment backed by action, and it had the result not only of improving Alcoa's reputation as a good place to work but of improving it across the board.

Other actions? In December 2000, Disney decided to discontinue use of its cartoon characters on cell phones, because of the often-expressed fear that the phones pose a health hazard. "Disney is the highest-profile company so far to take action to protect itself and its reputation in the event that cell phones are proved to be harmful," said a news report at the time.[15] When Unilever bought out Ben and Jerry's, the big food conglomerate was faced with the challenge of maintaining the little ice-cream company's commitment to social change and environmental protection; otherwise it would risk losing the very cachet (and intangible value!) that it was buying. After some prodding from company cofounder Ben Cohen, Unilever supported his proposal for a $5-million venture-capital fund aimed for businesses in low-income neighborhoods.[16] It also launched programs— tied to new ice-cream flavors—of making contributions to a children's playground-building organization and to scholarships for students at historically black colleges.[17]

5. Communicate. Press releases, image advertising, awards and grants, speeches by the CEO—all the tried-and-true forms of business communication—can help build reputation. But often it's more effective to branch out a little. Who are your company's allies? Its biggest critics? Monsanto formed its advisory committee. Some timber companies have sought out environmental groups, just to hear what they had to say and to explore the possibility of a partnership. Compaq Computer went so far as to seek out the creator of a Web site called whateveryoudodontbuyacompaq.com. "We had several dialogues," said Barry Bates, a senior manager of information and analysis for quality and customer care, "where a member of our team in a customer advocate role helped bring this guy around. Now, after almost a year, he has been added to our preproduct launch distribution. We send him the products—he 'kicks the tires'—just to get his feedback. He doesn't have the Web site up any longer. He's now—not necessarily an advocate, but at least someone with a voice and a level of expertise that we want to listen to."

Reputation can help you and it can destroy you. The difference is management. There is a market for information about reputations—whether it's on restroom walls or in sophisticated risk-adjustment models. And there is always someone who can benefit from spreading—or trafficking—in information about how you are doing. Perhaps even more than in most intangibles markets, this one will move whether you contribute to it or not. An entire field of academic research called "behavioral economics" is devoted to the study of the "psychology of markets." Managements that ignore the power of these currents are denying themselves a potent channel for good—and a terrible force for ill.

As this book was emerging from the final editing process, the Enron scandal broke in all of its sordid luminescence. As we re-read the chapter above, its importance becomes even clearer, particularly in light of the Enron situation. The company's swift destruction at the hands of the markets was driven relentlessly by the failure of its leaders to consider the impact of their actions on the capital markets' assessment of intangibles like leadership, brand, human capital and, of course, reputation. That assessment, in turn, led to a shut off of lending, denial of access to additional sources of funding, shunning by former friends in government and politics, and the inevitable filing under Chapter 11 of the US Bankruptcy Code.

A fuller examination of the role of intangibles will have to await the outcome of Congressional investigations and trials. However, two issues emerge. First, Enron illustrates the failure of the current system of corporate disclosure. The company's filings—aside from their apparently fraudulent nature—reported nothing new or innovative. Second, greater transparency in the form of disclosure about intangibles might well have signaled investors, regulators, and employees that all was not what it seemed.

NETWORKS AND ALLIANCES

10

*In the age of networks, it is impossible to do every-
thing on one's own.*

—Nobuyuki Idei,
CEO of Sony Corporation[1]

What would a Rip Van Winkle who had slept even just the past
decade make of some of the alliances, partnerships, and business networks that have cropped up in the last few years?

- Celera Genomics Corporation, a New York Stock Exchange
  company, announces a partnership with the National
  Institute of Health, including a $58-million grant from the
  National Institutes of Health to Celera and Baylor College
  of Medicine to sequence the genome of the laboratory rat.
  This follows a decade of bitter rivalry and animosity between the two organizations, both of which were working
  on decoding the human genome. The rivalry includes one
  episode in which the director of NIH's Center for Human
  Genome Research, Francis Collins, charges that Celera's
  techniques are so sloppy that the resulting genome map
  will read like a "*Mad* magazine."[2]

- Vivendi Universal—a global film-and-entertainment company that is part of what used to be a French water-distri-
  bution company (see chapter sixteen)—announces a
  global marketing alliance with automaker giant Toyota
  Motor Corporation. "The deal will result in Toyota spon-
  soring theme-park rides, placing its cars in Universal
  movies, and distributing, via Toyota dealership, special
  promotional CDs filled with Universal music," says a news
  report.[3]
- The Big Three automakers begin divesting themselves of
  large-parts divisions, including Delco Remy and Delphi
  (General Motors) and Visteon (Ford). The divisions can
  now sell to any customer. GM partners with seventeen suppliers to build an auto-manufacturing complex in Brazil,
  where GM itself will perform only final assembly operations. One partner is Fiat, with which GM plans to co-
  manufacture powertrains and transmissions for its Celta
  model. Fiat itself manufactures the Celta's top competitor,
  the Fiat Uno.[4]
- A once-sleepy suburban area to the west of Philadelphia has
  become home to dozens of new biotech companies. Not far
  away—in the Philadelphia and nearby New Jersey areas—
  is a concentration of big pharmaceutical companies and
  pharmaceutical manufacturing facilities. Specialized enterprises supplying these industries, such as manufacturing-
  engineering firms and pharmaceuticals-packaging companies, have moved in as well. Result: A declining manufacturing region has been transformed into a bustling center
  of high technology.

Alliances and networks between and among companies are as old
as business itself. The merchants of the Italian Renaissance set up
partnerships both to generate capital for their ventures and to lay off

some of the risk. The joint-stock companies of seventeenth-century England did much the same. In modern times, alliances of various sorts have gone in and out of favor. Multi-industry conglomerates—alliances carried to the extreme—were the rage of the 1960s. (Remember Harold Geneen's International Telephone and Telegraph? Or Charles Bluhdorn's Gulf & Western, known by the nickname Engulf & Devour?) More recently, consolidation among companies in the same industry has been fashionable in financial services, health care, entertainment, and a few other industries, although not always to the benefit of the shareholders of the consolidating companies.

But there's a longer-term, more durable trend that has taken shape over the last decade, and that seems likely to continue. Sony's Nobuyuki Idei calls it "soft alliances" as opposed to the "hard alliances" of a merger or consolidation. (Sony may have learned the value of such alliances the hard way: Its technically superior Betamax videotape format was overwhelmed by an alliance of manufacturers that effectively established VHS as the standard format for home VCRs.) Such alliances are the coin of the realm in the Intangibles Economy. According to one estimate, one-fifth of all revenue generated by the world's largest 1,000 companies comes from partnerships.[5] According to another, the top 500 global corporations average sixty major strategic alliances apiece.[6] Whatever the exact numbers, there's no doubt that partnerships, alliances, and networks of various sorts have grown both in number and in importance.

Soft alliances take several forms. One version is the kind of close supplier-customer relationship that Dell Computer has developed into an art form, and that the auto companies are now trying to cultivate. A second is partnerships among companies in unrelated fields, such as Vivendi Universal–Toyota (which resembles the longstanding marketing partnership between McDonald's and Walt Disney). A third version: temporary, shifting alliances even with one's competitors, as in the Fiat-GM example. Entertainment giants AOL Time Warner and Viacom are arch competitors, but they are also important suppliers and customers to each other through the web of television, film, and music companies that each controls.

Another sort of alliance—the kind of industrial network that has come to be known as a cluster and is typified by the Philadelphia biotech example—is growing in importance as well. Research led by Harvard Business School professor Michael E. Porter has identified literally hundreds of industrial clusters around the world, from the leather-fashion districts of Italy to the wine-producing regions of California. "Clusters encompass an array of linked industries and other entities important to competition," writes Porter. "They include, for example, suppliers of specialized inputs such as components, machinery, and services, and providers of specialized infrastructure. Clusters also often extend downstream to channels and customers and laterally to manufacturers of complementary products and to companies in industries related by skills, technologies, or common inputs."[7] Pathbreaking research on Silicon Valley by University of California professor AnnaLee Saxenian in the early 1990s found that companies in such a cluster engage in shifting patterns of competition and collaboration, allying themselves with partners on particular projects as opportunities arise.[8] The rise (and subsequent fall) of various "silicon" regions such as Silicon Glen (Scotland), Silicon Alley (New York City), and Silicon Prairie (Austin, Texas) attest to the strength of this concept. "Hollywood," "Wall Street," and "Inside the Beltway" (Washington, D.C., also known as "This Town," as in "he has a tough reputation in This Town") are other semi-mythical-but-thriving geographically based industry clusters.

THE POWER OF ALLIANCES

Why do alliances work? At the heart of the trend is the fact that not many companies these days do many things well. General Electric apart, conglomerates are no longer in fashion. Financial markets typically place more value on companies that focus on one kind of technology, one segment of the market, or one part of the value chain. The reasons aren't hard to fathom. In a hypercompetitive economy, no company can do everything better than its competitors. (The title of a popular 2001 business book by our CGEY colleague Fred Crawford was *The Myth of Excellence: Why Great Companies Never Try to Be the Best at Everything.*) In an economy that prizes and rewards innovation—and penalizes those who do not innovate—no company can stay at the leading edge in more than one or two fields.

Companies that focus thus learn to outperform their competitors. Southwest outperforms other airlines in part because it doesn't try to compete with them in long-haul, hub-and-spoke routes. Mobil decided to focus on the marketing end of the oil business, and came up with innovations such as the Speedpass quick-pay system. Companies that necessarily have a broad product line, such as the automakers, find that they must focus in a different way, by concentrating on one or two segments of the value chain—in their case, final assembly and marketing. Some companies realize late in the game that they should have focused their efforts much earlier. Until early 2001, the Japanese company Sega was a video-game machine manufacturer; its Dreamcast competed with Sony's PlayStation and Nintendo Corporation's Game Boy Advance. But Sega's machines did not sell well. Inventory built up, and the company was facing huge losses. So Sega's CEO Isao Okawa and COO Hideki Sato embarked on a new strategy: Discontinue the hardware, and focus instead on Sega's strong line of game titles. Henceforth, Sato announced, the company would make games for the PlayStation, Game Boy Advance, Microsoft's Xbox console, and Nintendo's GameCube, in addition to Dreamcast.[9]

But focused companies face a problem: limited opportunities for growth. Most can expand only so far in their chosen niches. To keep revenues and earnings on an upward curve, thereby satisfying the market, companies need to enter new markets and otherwise broaden their reach. That's where alliances come in: They offer growth opportunities combined with less exposure to risk. Thus GM is positioning itself to take advantage of what it hopes will someday be a booming car market in Brazil, without spending all the money necessary to build an auto-manufacturing complex—and without even hiring all the employees, most of whom will be on suppliers' payrolls. Electronics companies can launch new products without building new factories, simply by taking advantage of the large and booming contract-manufacturing industry. Amazon.com's partnership with Toys "R" Us helped both companies grow. Toys "R" Us had failed miserably in its own e-commerce efforts in 1999; because it underestimated the popularity of its Web site, thousands of gifts failed to arrive on time. Amazon.com, on the other hand, wrote off $34 million in toys that could not sell after the holiday season.[10] In 2000, thanks to its partnership with Amazon, Toys "R" Us's site became the most heavily trafficked site of the season—five times its nearest competitor—and allowed the company to do $180 million in business. Remarkably, even the Borders Group is now partnering with Amazon. Book sales on Borders's site will be run by Amazon, and Borders will get a share of revenue for the use of its name and customer base. Ed Wilhelm, Borders Group chief financial officer and senior vice president, said that the Internet "is definitely part of the future, and the choice is to build capabilities on your own or partner with someone who has already developed them."[11]

Two examples of successful alliances—one well known and well established, the other only now coming to fruition—illustrate the tremendous advantages that can be created by this intangible.

Wintel

The so-called Wintel alliance between Microsoft ("Win" for Windows) and Intel is a story so familiar that we take it for granted; yet it is a lesson often ignored.

Think back to 1980. The personal computer was a new concept. The industry leader was Apple Corporation, maker of the popular Apple II. Intel's primary business was memory chips; it had only recently developed the microprocessor. Microsoft was a thirty-two-employee company in the Seattle area that was writing software languages for PCs. When IBM decided to enter the business, it set up a separate operation in Boca Raton, Florida. Rather than developing and building all the key parts and software in-house, as "Big Blue" usually did, the new division would buy as many components as possible from outside suppliers.

In microprocessors, IBM's choice came down to Motorola versus Intel. The Motorola 68000 processor—used in Apple machines—was technologically superior, but the Intel 8086 chip was cheaper. IBM gave Intel the contract, and Intel developed the 8088 chip that would become the standard microprocessor on IBM's early models. The choice of Microsoft to build the operating system was more of an accident. IBM engineers paid a visit to Gary Kildall, head of a company called Digital Research Inc. DRI, as it was known, made an operating system called CP/M (Control Program for Microprocessors) that was widely used on non-Apple computers. But Kildall was out of the office and never met with the people from IBM. Next IBM contacted Bill Gates, who agreed to develop a system for IBM's new computer. He bought the rights to a CP/M-like program developed by Tim Patterson of Seattle Computer Products. Then he hired Patterson himself. Patterson, Gates, and Microsoft's other programmers adapted and expanded the operating system to accommodate IBM's plans. The result was MS-DOS, the first operating system built around the Intel 8088.

Microsoft retained the right to license versions of its operating system to others. When Compaq Computer reverse-engineered IBM's PC—and offered it to the market at a fraction of the price, thus becoming one of the fastest-growing companies in history—it, too, utilized Intel's chips and Microsoft's operating system. Soon other "IBM clones" were using them as well, and Wintel was on its way to becoming a standard. Standards, it should be noted, are created by alliances. Like Sony, which solely developed and marketed its Betamax format, Apple Computer utilized proprietary operating systems. Just as the

VHS format beat out Beta, so did MS-DOS machines beat out Apples. The only reason was that more companies were making them.

Still, PC hardware and software during the 1980s and '90s were by no means set in stone. IBM designed its own operating systems, OS/1 and OS/2, and tried hard to market them. Apple, too, fought back hard, bringing out innovative products based on Motorola chips. Other companies looked toward the UNIX operating system, and to different kinds of processors (for example, RISC chips). What kept the Wintel alliance on top was relentless innovation. Intel gave up its memory-chip business to focus on microprocessors, and came out with generation after generation of more powerful chips. Microsoft offered a suite of application software—Word, Excel, and others—designed specifically to work with its operating system. It brazenly copied many of the features of Apple's Macintosh, including the famous graphical user interface, incorporated them in the Windows version of its operating system, and then proceeded to update and improve Windows. Ironically, the whole thing was helped along by Intel's competition from Advanced Micro Devices (AMD). When AMD introduced its 386DX chip in 1992, the move touched off a price war; chip prices fell 40 to 50 percent, and the retail price of PCs followed them downward. That expanded the market by as much as one-third, and established Wintel as the dominant player for the years to come.

Biotech-Pharmaceuticals

When the biotech industry first got off the ground, in the 1980s, a few of the new companies had grand aspirations: They would be the next generation of pharmaceutical companies. They built manufacturing plants. They laid plans to test and market the drugs they were developing. Industry leaders such as Genentech attracted millions in venture capital and created a dramatic buzz when they went public. Soon, though, the appeal faded. Some of the drugs under development didn't live up to expectations. Others took much longer to develop than anyone had imagined. Market values collapsed, and some smaller biotech companies went under. Others sold ownership fractions to established pharmaceutical companies; the Roche Group, for instance, now owns 58 percent of Genentech.[12] Only a few biotech companies of that generation managed to survive as independents.

In the 1990s, the situation began changing. Biotechnology as a science continued to make enormous progress, the eventual decoding of the human genome being just one example. New companies were created to pursue new research findings. The pharmaceutical business was changing as well. Traditionally, most large drug firms had survived and prospered by finding and marketing "blockbusters"—drugs that could generate $1 billion or more in revenue every year. But it was getting both more expensive and more time-consuming to create such megadrugs. The pharmaceuticals began establishing new and lucrative alliances with biotech firms—and the biotech companies were now viewed more as partners than as objects for acquisition. "The harbinger of this trend was a deal in 1993, when SmithKline Beecham agreed to fork over a whopping $125 million for access to Human Genome Sciences' genomics data," journalist Brian O'Reilly reported.

In 1997 the trend began in earnest; Millennium Pharmaceuticals signed a record-setting $343-million agricultural-genomics alliance in 1997 with Monsanto. Ever bigger deals followed: a $465-million deal between Millennium and Bayer in 1998; an $815-million deal between Vertex Pharmaceuticals and Novartis in 2000. In 2001CuraGen Corporations's billion-dollar alliance with Bayer took the big/bio tango to a new level. Announced in January, the agreement shows more clearly than any deal to date how well-capitalized biotech companies, turbocharged by genomics, can now negotiate with big drug companies as equals, rather than as poor small cousins coming begging. Bayer and CuraGen will share up to $1.34 billion in drug development costs over fifteen years, with Bayer bearing 56 percent and CuraGen 44 percent. Unlike in Bayer's earlier deal with Millennium, Bayer and CuraGen will act as joint development partners—they'll share profits from the drugs they develop at the 56 to 44-percent ratio.[13]

Big drug firms were also partnering with biotech startups. "The biotechs are almost becoming a farm system for the big pharmaceutical companies," said Max Wallace, chief executive of Cogent Neuroscience, a biotech company located in North Carolina's Research Triangle Park looking for ways to stop brain cells from dying after a stroke.[14]

MANAGING ALLIANCES

Alliances present risks as well as opportunities; in fact, they often fail outright. A survey of 150 alliances by Vantage Partners, a Boston consulting firm, found that three-quarters were "failing or underperforming."[15] An in-depth study of 200 corporations and their 1,572 alliances by Jeffrey H. Dyer of Brigham Young University and his colleagues found that about half fail.[16] Some end in bitter squabbling; others are quietly discontinued. The result is the same: ineffectiveness. The Wintel alliance, for instance, was so successful in part because an ill-defined competing alliance around the Unix operating system was never able to iron out differences among the individual companies making up the alliance.

How can companies avoid failure? And how can they capitalize on the potential advantage an alliance creates? Once again, the key is to manage other critical intangibles. For example:

Leadership

An alliance ultimately requires collaboration between leaders of two or more companies—in some cases the CEOs, in others the heads of the relevant divisions. Alliances can founder on ego or personality clashes between these people. Even if the CEO is not directly involved, he or she can provide the alliance with both tangible and intangible support, or not. "Research reveals that compatibility of the

CEOs of the partner firms is essential to success," write William Q. Judge and Joel A. Ryman in a study of alliances in the U.S. healthcare industry.[17]

Strategy Execution

Just as mergers often founder on the rocks of poor execution, so do alliances. The recent alliances between U.S. and European airlines, for example, looked great—on paper. The companies, however, had neglected one important facet of the collaboration. In the United States, pilots earn top dollar, and regularly engage in collective bargaining to push their salaries still higher. European and Asian pilots, relatively underpaid, thought it appropriate that they should be paid on the same scales as their new alliance partners. The result: a spate of strikes, threatened strikes, and work slowdowns.

Communication

"Our problems with alliances have stemmed mainly from communications," said the vice president for product and technology management at Ryder Systems. "We're a $5.5 billion company with many operating locations around the world. We could overwhelm our [partners] by having 50 people calling them at once." Ryder believes it has solved its problems by channeling communications through two people, a manager and a technical specialist, who act as points of contact.[18]

Culture

Biotech and pharmaceutical companies have vastly different cultures, and alliance partners have had to work hard to overcome the differences. High-tech companies on the West and the East Coasts of the United States have equally different cultures. "We tend to focus on a few things excessively," said Beau Vrolyk, former senior vice president of the computer-systems business unit at Silicon Graphics, based in California; he acknowledged that he might hold a meeting, for example, at 9:30 P.M. Few New Englanders would put up with such a schedule.[19]

Innovation

Wintel succeeded because of Microsoft's and Intel's commitment to innovation. An alliance among Group Health Cooperative of Puget Sound, health-products distributor Owens & Minor, and 3M Health Care came up with an innovative plan by which the HMO would purchase medical and surgical supplies on a "capitation" basis—that is, using a preset reimbursement amount for each type of medical procedure. The three companies agreed to share the proceeds if costs declined and to put up additional funds if costs rose. As it happened, costs declined 35 percent over three years, and the alliance was correspondingly strengthened.[20]

The tools for meeting such challenges aren't difficult to enumerate, though they are often hard to utilize:

- The leaders of allied companies must get to know one another, and establish a relationship of trust. "You can put only so much in the contract," says the MasterCard executive responsible for developing new markets.[21]
- Those responsible for the alliance must perform adequate due diligence into every facet of their proposed partner's operation that is likely to affect the alliance—especially including the partner's culture. Potential obstacles must be identified and laid out on the table for discussion.
- The partners in an alliance must also lay out the objectives they hope to accomplish, and agree on the metrics by which success is measured. A 1999 survey found that "only 51% of companies that form alliances had any kind of formal metrics in place to assess alliance performance." Of

those, moreover, "only 20% believed that the metrics they had in place were really the appropriate ones to use."[22]

- Specific people must be assigned responsibility for managing the relationship, with the understanding both that they will be supported by their employers and that they will be held responsible for the alliance's performance.

- Because managers may find themselves working with people who don't report to them, the skill known as "lateral management," or leading through persuasion rather than by issuing direct orders, is invaluable.

Alliances are not for the timid. The Vantage Partners/Harvard Negotiation Project study that found 75 percent of alliances fail noted that excitement about potential alliance synergies frequently masks conflicts between partners over trust, respect, and goals. Problems include hardball negotiations on the path to an agreement that breed lingering resentment and the increasingly delicate balancing act required of organizations that are allied in one aspect of their business but are bitter competitors in another. These obstacles are compounded by the absence, in alliances, of traditional structures so comforting to many managers. That said, the capital markets have spoken. Companies that achieve the efficiencies to be realized in resource allocation and executive attention are rewarded with higher Price/Earnings multiples—and better run businesses.

TECHNOLOGY
AND PROCESSES

*Technology costs for delivering a minute of voice
track to a customer are only about 7 percent of total
costs. It actually costs more to bill a customer today
than it does to provide the service to that customer.*

—John Sidgmore,
Vice Chairman, Worldcom, Inc.

How often we imbue technology with magical powers! We think that
investments in new machinery or information systems will somehow
magically boost productivity, shorten cycle time, cut costs, and accomplish a host of other objectives besides. We believe that products or
services—even whole companies—built around new technologies will
somehow magically find a market. Most such hopes, of course, are
shattered by cold doses of reality. The technology fails to live up to expectations. The dreams built around it vanish with the morning light.

And yet sometimes new technology actually does all that we expect
it to. Industries are transformed. Vast new markets are created.
Companies use technologies to change the way they do things. They
use technologies to offer their customers new products and services.
Sometimes they reap outsize rewards.

By now, the difference between technological failure and technological success shouldn't be a surprise: It lies in intangibles.

Technology itself may be a tangible investment, but everything around the technology—everything needed to make the technology do what it is supposed to do—is intangible. This chapter tells some tales of technology, which are both cautionary and inspiring, and explicates some of the intangibles that create the difference.

GM AND ROBOTICS

In the 1960s, a company called Unimation had created rudimentary robots to perform die-casting operations for General Motors. Though the results of this experiment were mixed, GM decided that robots were the wave of its future. The rising labor costs of the 1970s—and the looming threat of competition from overseas—made the adoption of robot technology seem even more urgent. Beginning in 1980 GM spent $42 billion re-equipping existing factories and building new ones.[1] Robots were an important part of this investment.

GM's new partner in robotics was the Japanese company Fanuc Ltd., a leader in its industry. Instead of developing robots to take over just one piece of the assembly process, GM and Fanuc created a line of robots that could both weld and paint. These robots could also sense light and touch, which gave them inspection and feedback capabilities as well as the ability to perform mechanical tasks. In GM's plan, unmanned mobile trucks called AGVs (automatic guided vehicles) would transport components to the robots, so that every "member" of the assembly line had the right amount of parts at the right time. Machine-controlled cameras and laser-based measuring systems would replace human quality control in many factories. An inter-robotic communication system known as MAP (manufacturing automation protocol) would allow machines to communicate their output and any system alerts to a "master control" computer. Eventually, GM hoped to have a computer-integrated manufacturing line (CIM), in which computers would help design, manufacture, and transport the product from start to finish.[2]

GM spent a half-billion dollars just at its Hamtramck plant in Detroit, which utilized 260 robots and 50 AGVs along with 42 workers spread over two shifts.[3] The company figured it would save money partly through the reduction of labor costs (45 percent over several years, according to the forecast) and partly through the reduction of middle management and quality-control expenses. Full automation, so GM hoped, would also reduce or even eliminate the burden of overstocked parts; the AGVs would provide "just-in-time" accurate delivery.

Alas, the experiment mostly failed. After two years of robotics, production levels at the plants involved had fallen dramatically. By 1989, GM's market share had dropped from 46 percent to 35 percent. In 1992 alone it lost more than $23 billion.[4] Robots were hardly the only, or even the major, cause of the company's troubles. But they didn't help, either.

WEBVAN: COLLAPSE OF A DOT-COM

Lest we imagine that such large investments in technology are a thing of the past, consider the experience of Webvan. Launched in 1996 by bookstore magnate Louis Borders, Webvan was the most ambitious of the online grocery merchants. It raised capital from blue-chip investors, including CBS, Knight-Ridder, and leading venture-capital funds. By June 1999, when it opened for business, the company employed 414 full-time and 259 part-time people in its Oakland, California, distribution center. From the beginning the company's Web site offered some 20,000 products, along with prepared meals. In its first four months of operation it recorded more than $4 million in sales.

In September 1999 Webvan hired a high-profile CEO—George Shaheen, the former CEO of Andersen Consulting. Later that year the company went public at $15 a share; the price rose quickly to nearly $25, giving Webvan a valuation of nearly $8 billion. Soon the company had expanded to seven other cities, and said that it would be in twenty-six within three years. In 2000 Webvan raised another $275 million from the capital markets and acquired Seattle-based competitor HomeGrocer. It began laying plans for adding books and videos to its product line.

The key to Webvan's business plan was advanced technology, which the company felt would lower its labor costs enough that it could take a large chunk of the fiercely competitive grocery business. Its Web site was big and complex, listing many thousands of products, and generally easy to use. Its fulfillment operations were to be state of the art. Webvan signed a $1-billion contract with Bechtel Inc., the giant construction firm, to build brand-new distribution centers at $25 million to $35 million each. Its flagship center, in Oakland, was large enough to service the equivalent of eighteen conventional supermarkets. Operations there—and in the few other centers the company actually built—were highly automated. For example:

- The order process was completely computerized. Orders were picked and packed in the distribution center and put into totes that were color-coordinated according to temperature requirements.
- Webvan's center "featured an intricate system of carousels and conveyors that routed the products to the employees rather than moving employees to the product. At any given time a picker moved no more than 19.5 feet in any direction and had access to over 8,000 bins of goods."
- Orders were taken from the distribution center to "docking stations" and reloaded onto smaller delivery trucks. Delivery drivers were equipped with wireless computers allowing them to communicate directly with the warehouse.[5]

Of course, none of the fancy technology made any difference. The market for online groceries didn't grow nearly as fast as Webvan (and a lot of other companies) expected. None of the distribution centers ever operated anywhere near capacity, which meant that the cost savings were evanescent. The company burned through its cash. Borders left the board. Shaheen resigned as CEO. In mid-2001 the company closed its doors.

EXECUTING A TECHNOLOGY-BASED STRATEGY

As we saw in chapter six, one key to success in the Intangibles Economy is a company's ability to execute its technology-based strategy. Both GM, in its robotics days, and Webvan, more recently, had a very clear strategy that they couldn't execute. The reason is simple: A strategy that relies primarily on unfamiliar or untested technology is the most difficult kind to execute that can be imagined. Indeed, history is littered with the casualties of misguided technologists. Thomas Edison very nearly came a cropper with his promotion of direct-current electricity generation and distribution; the alternating current favored by his rival George Westinghouse proved to be more practical. Electric utilities later in the twentieth century placed huge bets on the construction of nuclear-powered generating facilities, only to find that these facilities were riddled with safety and operational problems.

What's involved in execution of a technology-based strategy? At root, it's the realization that any technology has to mature—and that depends on people. Engineers must learn its possibilities and its characteristic troubles, and they must develop second- and third-generation versions. Entrepreneurs and other businesspeople must try out alternative technologies to see which ones turn out to be cost-effective. Customers must have a chance to familiarize themselves with the technology's operations—and then to decide whether or not they will adopt it. GM implemented its robotics program with an immature technology. The robots would not operate reliably in a manufacturing environment marked by changes in temperature and humidity. They broke down frequently. The robots were mixed and matched into many different systems, and adjustments to one often caused unexpected electrical shutdowns somewhere else.[6] Webvan staked its very existence on an untested technology—not the warehouses, which were simply expensive, but on large numbers of customers' willingness to place orders over the Web.

Companies that learn this lesson—companies that experiment with new technologies as they are maturing, that place small bets and learn from the results—can capitalize on the new possibilities a technology creates. Take the Web. Amidst the collapse of the dot-coms, plenty of companies are learning to utilize just the kind of on-line ordering and high-tech order fulfillment that proved to be Webvan's undoing. Industrial suppliers such as Parker Hannifin and W. W. Grainger now conduct a sizable fraction of their transactions over the Web; so do numerous consumer-goods companies. Online travel agencies such as Travelocity and Expedia are both profitable; in the quarter ending June 20, 2001, for instance, Expedia earned $15 million on $78.5 million in revenue. But take note: Though you might want to invest in a travel agency that focuses on selling airline tickets over the Web, you wouldn't want to invest in one that sells cruise tickets. Consumers have shown that they are happy to comb through databases in search of cheap airfares. But when they're booking a cruise, they like a travel agent to walk them through the various complex alternatives. Jupiter Media Metrix, an Internet market-research firm in New York, estimated that just 1.3 percent of U.S. cruise booking would be done online in 2001, compared with 13 percent of U.S. airline bookings. By 2004, Jupiter expects that the portion of airline bookings handled online will climb to 21 percent, compared to 3.6 percent of cruises.[7]

Certainly the events of September 11, 2001, adversely affected the online travel industry. On September 10 of that year, Richard Barton, chief executive of Expedia, Inc., was prepared to announce that just two quarters after posting its first profit, the agency was likely to be $10 million above their target of $80 million. However, in the three weeks following the tragedy, Expedia Inc.'s revenues came up $10 million short, reducing profits from $10.1 million to $6.1 million, but still allowing Expedia to post its third consecutive quarter of profitability in the quarter ending September 30, 2001. Expedia transaction volumes as of mid-October were at 85 percent of pre–September 11 levels. As *BusinessWeek* put it, "While the A-team players have bright prospects long term, a short economic downturn could slow profit growth for such players as Expedia, travel agent Travelocity.com, name-your-price site Priceline.com, and real estate site Homestore.com. A long recession could make a number of profitable companies profitless again."[8] However, some travel sites continue to announce continued growth overall. On November 14, 2001, Orbitz, the travel site launched by American, Continental, Delta, Northwest, and United Airlines, announced that their site traffic peaked in October when 6.3 million unique users visited the site, up from a reported 4 million in September. They also reported that gross travel bookings and sales transactions hit all-time highs for the first week in November 2001. Travelocity reported that stock as of mid-November 2001 was trading at 80 percent of pre–September 11 levels. This points out that it's hard to generalize about technological advances, even after a dramatic incident such as the one on September 11, without looking at the related intangibles.

Much the same kind of step-by-step progress can be seen in the area of factory automation, which now generally goes under the rubric "e-manufacturing." A Delphi Automotive Systems injection-molding plant in Cortland, Ohio, for instance, has 120 presses that crank out a billion plastic housings for electric connectors every year. The plant is overseen by a network that monitors individual machines, tools, finished parts, and shipping, even allowing the plant manager to check on operations from his PC at home. The network "alerts operators when something is wrong with a machine—before it starts spitting out defective parts or shuts down completely. It tells suppliers when to restock the plant's inventory and lets customers know exactly when their order will arrive."[9] Delphi has spent only about $44 million on the system, or about one-tenth of 1 percent of what GM spent on robots. Because the information technology it utilizes has matured, the company was able to stitch the system together mostly from existing well-tested components, including Microsoft Windows NT, Oracle databases, Compaq servers, and software from GE Fanuc. This allowed engineers to debug the system effectively when the inevitable glitches occurred.

What about the famous first-mover advantage, which rewards companies that take big risks first? Sometimes the advantage is real—and sometimes those pioneers really do get the big rewards. More often than not, however, it's the more patient company that learns to capitalize on a new technology, by conducting smaller-scale experiments and learning, gradually, to execute a technology-based strategy.

THE HUMAN SIDE OF TECHNOLOGY

The other major point we'd like to make about technology in the Intangibles Economy is this: Successful investment in technology requires investment in a host of other intangibles, notably work processes, human capital, and workplace organization. Technology alone rarely provides a company with a competitive edge. Technology complemented by investments in intangibles does—or at least it can.

Work Processes

Every time a new technology comes along, it seems, people at first expect it to do no more and no less than replace some existing technology. That was certainly the case with electric motors. In the nineteenth century, factories were typically powered by a water or steam engine. In both cases, the power was generated at a central location and then distributed throughout the factory by a complicated system of belts, shafts, and gearwheels. Individual machines had no power of their own; to work, they had to be connected to a spinning shaft. When electric motors first became available, what could be more natural than to think that giant motors would replace the water or steam? Indeed, the first electrified factories operated on just such a principle.

From our vantage point, it's easy to see how limited an improvement this was. The factory still needed its mechanical power-distribution system, which constrained both its architecture and its operation. It was still vulnerable both to failures in the distribution system and to failures in the central power source. Flexibility was greatly limited; machines could be added or reconfigured only with enormous difficulty. When fractional-horsepower electric motors became available, machine makers and their customers slowly—slowly!—realized that it was ultimately far more efficient and reliable to do away with belts and shafts and to install wiring throughout the factory, then power each machine with its own motor. It was literally decades, however, before most U.S. factories had made the changeover.

At GM, the robots were seen purely as a replacement technology; each one took the place of a worker or group of workers. But a robot and a worker are quite different; each has capabilities the other doesn't. Before robots were ever introduced, the work process itself needed to be reengineered to take advantage of robots' special capabilities (faster production) and to protect against the robot's limitations (for example, the fact that it will blindly follow instructions even if the instructions are bad). In a similar vein, many brick-and-mortar companies reacted to the rise of the Internet by incorporating order-taking capabilities into their Web sites. But when an order came in over the Web, it was then hand-processed as if it had just come in by fax or telephone. The Web was treated purely as a replacement technology, and the gains in speed or efficiency were virtually zero. (Needless to say, Webvan did not make this mistake.)

Part of the immense appeal of business-process reengineering in the 1990s lay in companies' realization that work processes did indeed have to be altered to take advantage of new technologies. In a classic example described by reengineering proponents Michael

Hammer and James Champy, the work process at IBM Credit, which financed the purchase of mainframe computers, was "positively Dickensian." An inquiry about financing came first to an order taker, who then logged the request for the deal on a piece of paper. Someone walked the slip of paper upstairs, where the information was entered into a computer system. The business practices department then modified the standard loan agreement as necessary and sent the request to a pricer. The pricer determined the appropriate interest rate and sent the material on to a clerical group to be written up. The process took between six days and two weeks. Obviously it made no sense to "automate" each person's work, even if that were possible; instead the whole process had to be rebuilt, so that one generalist did the work of several specialists. IBM Credit did just that—and in the process cut its turnaround time to four hours. [10]

Workplace Organization

But look what happens when you reengineer in this manner: Suddenly people are expected to make decisions that they didn't have to make in the past. ("At the points in the process where workers used to have to go up the managerial hierarchy for an answer, they now make their own decisions," write Hammer and Champy.)[11] In other words, jobs and responsibilities change. Hence the importance of coupling new technology with training, discussion, and other tools designed to get employees to buy in to the new technology. Some years ago, when U.S. Steel installed a new continuous caster at its Edgar Thomson Works in Braddock, Pennsylvania, it not only spent more than $8 million training 200-plus steelworkers how to operate it, it also set up teams and work groups charged with establishing their own goals and measuring their own performance. "The person making a living as a steelworker is the person who can let us know how to be more productive," a manager at the plant told a reporter. "That is a change in management that came along with the caster."[12]

For its part, GM was evidently clumsy in its introduction of robots, failing to involve workers in the change to the new technology. But GM learned from its experience. In 1984, it joined Toyota to set up a company called New United Motor Manufacturing Inc. (NUMMI), in Fremont, California. The plant—an old one owned by GM—was placed under Toyota's management, and the cars produced were to be divided between the two companies and sold under two different brand names, Toyota Corolla and Geo Prizm. To GM's surprise, Toyota declined to use robotics. Instead, it divided the workers into teams without classified jobs and gave them power to control the assembly line when problems were detected. The result: a production level as high as GM's projected production level in its automated plant.[13] When GM built its Saturn plant in Spring Hill, Tennessee, it was mindful of the NUMMI experience. Saturn's planners emphasized collaboration among designers, engineers, and assembly workers. The collaborative teams sorted out potential problems before beginning production. Only 200 robots were employed in the entire production process, and they were used only for welding. The plant's 5,000 workers—who used conventional transport methods of electrified monorail, conveyor belts, and lift trucks—were divided into teams of six to fifteen people, with each team deciding its own training needs and task assignments.[14] Since the first Saturn was sold in 1990, the brand has enjoyed an excellent sales record and top marks in quality.

Professor Erik Brynjolfsson and his colleagues at MIT's Sloan School of Business have studied companies' investments in information technologies, and have found that they are almost invariably accompanied by much larger investments in intangibles such as those mentioned. Companies that invest heavily in IT, he says, "are also more likely to adopt work practices that involve a cluster of organizational characteristics, including greater use of teams, broader decision-making authority, and increased worker training." These characteristics, moreover, increase a firm's market value over and above what can be accounted for by its investment in computer technology. "We conclude that investors believe that the contribution of computers is increased when they are combined with certain intangible assets, specifically including the cluster of organizational changes that we have identified."[15]

7-ELEVEN

Today, information technology has reached a point where it can be utilized effectively (though not every company does so). People are familiar with it, and know that it doesn't necessarily threaten their jobs. Complementary technologies such as communications have evolved in lockstep with information processing itself. Moreover—thanks in part, it must be said, to reengineering—companies have learned that information systems are good for much more than automating existing processes; they can help the business modify its strategy to create whole new sources of value for customers. A case in point is 7-Eleven.

Founded in 1927, 7-Eleven is the world's largest operator, franchisor, and licensor of convenience stores, with more than 21,000 units worldwide. It's also one of the United States's largest independent gasoline retailers. It pioneered the convenience store concept during its first years of operation as an ice company; its retail outlets began selling milk, bread, and eggs as a convenience to customers. Today, it faces many of the same challenges as other retailers: watching demographics and consumer tastes, keeping up with technology. In the late 1990s the 7-Eleven chain committed itself to a four-year revitalization period aimed at staving off competition from grocery stores, fast-food chains, and other convenience stores. Its goal is to become a modern marketplace offering fresh products at good value with unbeatable convenience.

The watchwords of this new strategy are freshness, speed, and variety. Each 7-Eleven location tries to maintain a selection of 2,500 different products, tailored to meet the needs and preferences of local customers. Stores are being remodeled to add more light and space, and to allow electronic monitoring of the entire area for safety. Distribution centers are being established to deliver fresh foods such as pastries, fruits, and yogurts on schedule or on demand. In addition, 7-Eleven offers consumers services designed to meet the unique needs of individual neighborhoods, including automated money orders, copiers, fax machines, automatic teller machines, phone cards, and (where available) lottery tickets.

In service of the strategy, 7-Eleven has also adopted a series of technological improvements[16]:

- Punch-key registers are being replaced by touch-screen semiautomated systems, large buttons, and simple logic adapted to the 7-Eleven workforce, which turns over rapidly and includes a large number of recent immigrants. The new screens minimize the use of English. They also allow customer purchases to be processed more quickly, thus permitting high traffic volumes.
- Inventory processing by hand and paper is giving way to an RIS (retail information system) connected to the registers, back room, distribution centers, and headquarters. As at Wal-Mart, the system can tally the inflow and outflow of products for each store in real time.
- The same system allows detailed sales and inventory forecasts. It will calculate (for example) what proportion of customers buys donuts, and how many donuts the store should keep available. If the proportion of donut-buyers suddenly drops, the system can help answer the question of whether the donut quality is too low, the price is too high, or the store's selection is not what the customers wanted.
- The new 7-Eleven store network (Intranet) keeps store managers informed of local weather conditions, traffic congestion, community events, and promotions by its suppli-

ers. The information helps the manager make staffing, supply, and pricing decisions.

All this technology isn't being introduced in a vacuum. The company hopes to keep its employees up to date on new products with its annual "University of 7-Eleven." Classes are open for about 700 people from Texas's 7-Eleven stores to enable managers and other employees to become more familiar with the company's products so they can be more helpful to customers.[17]

Technology investments can be productive, but only if the organization doing the investing makes the corresponding investments in intangibles—people and processes—that are necessary. On a modest scale, 7-Eleven may be doing just that.

The harsh reality is that technology is a mixed blessing, a two-faced idol like the gods of ancient civilizations who were both creators and destroyers. It can accelerate your growth and then multiply in a flash the negative effects of that same phenomenon. Our research, and that of others, suggests that the largest benefits in increasing technology investments come from those targeted at areas that may be invisible to consumers but are likely to have a major effect on quality, price, and service.[18] The potential gains or losses a company may realize from technology investments are virtually limitless. Intangibles play *the* crucial role in deciding which it will be. They are the differentiators that mitigate the risk of making the wrong decision or enhance the benefits of making the right one. The world is full of brilliant new ideas. It's knowing how to put them to work that is the key to successful decision-making.

HUMAN CAPITAL

We spend all our time on people. The day we screw
up the people thing, this company is over.

—Jack Welch, former CEO,
General Electric Company

Do people matter to a business? Everybody knows they do, and more so in the Intangibles Economy than ever before. Just look at all the companies that call their employees "associates" or "partners." Look at the companies that still offer unusual perks such as concierge services and paid sabbaticals, in hopes of making themselves into a so-called employer of choice. And listen to all the CEOs who regularly declare, "Our People Are Our Most Important Assets."

Unfortunately this is a truth often observed in the breach. When markets turn down, companies race to slash their payrolls—and Wall Street usually rewards them for it. In the first five months of 2001 alone, U.S. companies announced more than 650,000 job cuts.[1] Between September 11 and mid-November 2001, the *Washington Post* online listed over 400,000 layoffs in eleven industries, the largest being the airline industry, reporting over 120,000 job cuts.[2] Even in good times, many employees are less than satisfied with their jobs. In a 1999 survey, for example, 33 percent of employees were "not committed to their present employer and not planning to stick around another two years." Another 39 percent were "trapped"—they said that they were planning to stay, but they didn't feel committed to their employer.[3] Evidently these people didn't feel like anybody's most important asset.

To understand this contradiction, companies must learn to actively manage the cluster of intangibles that make up their human capital.

THE DESKILLING—AND RESKILLING—OF PEOPLE

In the earliest wood- and metalworking factories, companies depended mightily on the skills of their workers. Parts were manufactured only to broad tolerances and had to be shaped or filed by hand to fit. Machines were largely put together by hand as well; making them work right was a job for skilled, experienced assemblers.[4] But such a system put serious constraints on a business. Growth was limited by the supply of skilled workers. If one employee left, a company might need months to find and train a new one. Profits, too, could be constrained by these workers' demands for higher wages. The earliest unions were craft unions representing highly skilled employees—in some ways not so different from medieval guilds.

Over time, not surprisingly, companies worked hard at deskilling factory work. Inspired by thinkers such as Frederick W. Taylor, they designed work processes so that more and more work could be done by the unskilled labor that was so plentiful at the time. Better machine tools produced parts that were interchangeable in fact as well as in theory. These parts could be bolted or screwed together by assemblers who needed no more than an hour or two of training. The new approach increased productivity; it also allowed companies to grow rapidly, just by buying more machines and hiring more unskilled workers. Not incidentally, it increased management's power over employees. The workforce was fungible, in the sense that virtually any member of it could easily be replaced by someone else.

This model of management defined not only factory labor, but much white-collar and service work as well—and not just in the early part of the twentieth century. In the 1970s, for example, a journalist named Barbara Garson took a series of low-level jobs and reported her experiences in a book called *All the Livelong Day*. Listen to her account of work at an insurance company:

> *I worked for a while at the Fair Plan Insurance Company, where hundreds of women sat typing and breaking down sextuplicate insurance forms. My job was in endorsements.*
> *—First, third and fourth copies staple together/Place the pink sheet in back of the yellow/ If the endorsement shows a new mortgagee/ Stamp the fifth copy "certificate needed"—*
> *Other sections like coding, checks, filing and endorsement typing did similar subdivided parts of the paperwork. The women in the other sections sat at steel desks like mine, each working separately on a stack of forms or cards. Every section had a supervisor who counted and checked the work. She recorded the number of pieces we completed, and the number of errors we made, on our individual production sheets. . . . Aside from counting and checking the supervisors also tried to curtail talking and eating at the desks.*[5]

In many respects, work life in large companies wasn't so different even for managers. They occupied well-defined slots in the organizational chart. They reported up, managed down, and hoped to get promotions (along with a slightly larger office) every couple of years.

But with the vast changes in the economy (described in chapter two) came equally vast changes in the workplace. In effect, the deskilling of work was largely reversed. Three kinds of changes were particularly important.

What People Were Doing

The service sector grew enormously, and the service sector as a rule is more dependent on human skills than traditional manufacturing is. Take the hospitality industry. Much of the value incorporated in any one company is tangible—hotels, restaurants, kitchen equipment, furnishings, and so on. But much also resides in the skills and manners of desk clerks, room-service attendants, wait staff, cooks, and other employees. It's the same in many other service industries, whether or not they are capital-intensive in the conventional sense. Airlines necessarily rely heavily on the skilled labor of pilots, desk clerks, flight attendants, and mechanics. Financial services firms depend mightily on their fund managers, analysts, brokers, computer programmers, and customer-service representatives.

In a part of the service sector—call it the "brain" or the "talent" sector—nearly all the value resides in the heads of individual people. This sector includes sports, the arts, and entertainment, of course, but also legal services, accounting, some financial services, management consulting, architecture and design, advertising, software, IT consulting, and much of medicine, the media, and education. The importance of people in these businesses extends well beyond the few superstars that are in the public eye. A Tom Cruise or a Julia Roberts is worth millions to any movie project, to be sure. But cinematographers, set designers, supporting actors, casting specialists, editors, and many, many other highly skilled people are needed to make the finished product.

How They Were Doing It

The scene described by Barbara Garson in the 1970s seems almost as dated today as Charlie Chaplin's labor in *Modern Times*. Nor is it simply that the various tasks in Garson's office would now be computerized. As at IBM Credit—described in the previous chapter—companies have reengineered the workflow so that it is rarely as subdivided as it used to be; teams of generalists have largely replaced vast arrays of specialists. This is as true in manufacturing as it is in services such as insurance. More and more factories utilize team-based cellular-manufacturing systems, in which groups of employees work together to produce a product, each one doing a variety of tasks. A reengineering of a Maytag dishwasher plant in Tennessee along these lines boosted quality 55 percent, reduced work in progress 60 percent, and freed up 43,000 square feet of plant space.[6]

What Was Valued

In the industrial economy, what was valued was showing up for work, doing a good job, and not causing trouble. In the Intangibles Economy, that's no longer enough. Most companies expect workers at all levels to take initiative, offer suggestions, and solve problems. One example is Saturn Corporation, a wholly owned subsidiary of General Motors. Production employees there are expected to participate in making decisions that affect them, including process layout and sequence and interaction with other parts of the plant. They're also expected to assume responsibility for the quality of their output ("You go fix a problem that came from your team," as one former employee puts it). This, by the way, was one of the enduring lessons from world business's fascination with the "Japanese way." NUMMI, the San Francisco–area plant, put these lessons into practice. The plant introduced employee-empowered teams and other high-performance work practice innovations to reduce labor-management turmoil and increase production. In general, organizations can compete today only if they are continually improving and continually innovating. At Saturn, for instance, another innovative approach is in training, which is recognized as critical to the success of the organization and of the individual. Each employee is expected to spend 5 percent of overall working hours in training. If every employee (union and management) completes eighty hours of training in the year, an additional component is added to the year-end bonus.

The cumulative effects of these trends is a kind of reskilling of the workplace. People know more and are expected to do many more different kinds of things on the job than they were in the past. More companies depend more heavily on high-level skills and knowledge than in the past. This is what is meant by the phrase "knowledge economy" (though we believe that this particular phrase captures only a part of what is truly new in today's marketplace). What people know matters; hence who works for your company and how much they can learn matters as well. These intangible factors create the advantage in today's economy.

HUMAN CAPITAL AT WORK

Researchers have begun to quantify, in various ways, the effects of investment in human capital. For example:

- In our own Value Creation Index study, described in chapter seventeen, human capital consistently ranked as one of the top three drivers of intangible value.
- Consulting firm Watson Wyatt Worldwide studied 405 public companies and found that a well-managed workforce can add up to 30 percent to a company's market value.[7]
- In a study for the American Society for Training and Development, researchers ranked forty companies according to their average training expenditure per employee. Companies in the top half had higher net sales and higher gross profit per employee than those in the bottom half; they also had a higher market-to-book ratio and greater growth in market-to-book.[8]
- Studies of mergers and acquisitions uncover the fact—already known to many practitioners—that many founder on the rocks of people issues. "One common deal pitfall is not dealing with the 'softer' issues such as how the two organizations will fit together culturally and whether top talent will stay with the new company."[9]
- Former Harvard Business School professor David H. Maister studied twenty-nine professional service firms in fifteen countries to assess the relationship between em-

ployee attitudes and business success. His conclusion: Attitudes drive financial results. Raise employee satisfaction 20 percent, he argues, and a company can boost its financial performance more than 40 percent.

- A landmark study in 1994—following the last era of intensive job cuts—compared the financial performance of Fortune 100 companies over a five-year period, both before and after the announcement of workforce reductions. "Contrary to expectations, the results indicated that financial performance worsened, rather than improved, following announced layoffs."[10]

In a different vein entirely, AnnaLee Saxenian of the University of California, Berkeley, traced the impact on Silicon Valley of the immigration of Chinese and Indian engineers. This was "human capital" with a vengeance: 55 percent of the Indian and 40 percent of the Chinese engineers working in the Valley held advanced degrees, as compared to only 18 percent of white engineers. By 1998, Chinese and Indian engineers were leading nearly one-quarter of Silicon Valley high-technology businesses started between 1980 and 1998. These companies as a group accounted for more than $16.8 billion in sales and 58,282 jobs.[11]

MANAGING HUMAN CAPITAL

How can companies attract good people, keep them, help them develop their potential, and so make maximum use of the capital they represent?

The characteristic employment relationships of today's economy, it's safe to say, are still being worked out. Certainly they're likely to be less stable and less secure (at least at the white-collar level) than the characteristic one-company, one-career employment relationship of times past. During the boom of the 1990s, indeed, pundits urged people to think of themselves as "free agents" or as a "company of one," and to make short-term contracts with employers to do particular pieces of work. Employers, for their part, went to sometimes-absurd lengths to attract and keep full-time, long-term workers. (Remember the foosball tables and pet-sitting services?) As the boom cooled, the balance of power in the marketplace shifted. More people seemed to be wanting full-time work, and companies found that they had to offer less to attract and keep people.

The shifting balance of power in the labor market, however, obscured the real issues. In the Intangibles Economy, a company is in many respects only as good as its people. Factories and stores can be built or bought, business models copied, capital attracted. What distinguishes one organization from another is who works for it, how good they are, and how productively they can work together. Says Walter Wriston, the former CEO of Citicorp: "Successful corporate managers must know that the company's real competitors in the marketplace are not the ones that they have been familiar with for years, but that the vital competition is for men and women with the brains to survive and prosper. If all the brains go to one segment of the economy or to one company in your industry but not to yours, then it doesn't really matter what your competitors may be. You have already lost the race." So companies need to build and utilize their human capital regardless of economic conditions. They can do so using traditional tools—but also some nontraditional tools as well.

Recruitment

The day of simply putting an ad in the paper and waiting for job candidates to show up is past. At the least, the ad will now go into an Internet database as well as in the newspaper. But recruiters for successful companies know there's more to recruitment than that. They work the campuses for bright young people, often establishing relationships with (and getting recommendations from) key professors.

They network relentlessly at industry events, knowing that a competitor today can be a colleague tomorrow.

From our perspective, what's significant about recruiting is how much it depends on successful management of other intangibles. What is the company's reputation? How well does it communicate with the outside world? Can it boast the kind of high-performance workplace described in the next chapter? What does its brand stand for? Disney invites prospective theme-park hires into a "casting center" complete with a model of Snow White's castle.[12] General Motors in June 2001 invited its 1,800 student interns to drive its most exciting cars and trucks at the company's annual Student Summit. "There's no better way to stir the passion of future GM employees than by letting them take our products out for a drive," said global human resources vice president Katy Barclay. "And we hope that these students will strongly consider GM as the best place to apply their skills."[13] Other companies are investing in environmental programs and donating to charities as a way of making themselves more attractive employers.

The flip side of the equation is that the more companies depend on the skills and experience of their employees, the more they must evaluate the intangibles those potential recruits bring to the company. "A major league player is someone who has the ability to physically compete on that level," says Oakland Athletics baseball team assistant general manager Paul DePodesta. "A championship player has the physical ability as well as the mental capacity, the intensity, the competitiveness, all those intangibles that it really takes not just to succeed but to excel."

Compensation

Compensation all by itself is an intangible that seems to have significant effects on performance. One study by a major human-resources consulting firm estimates that 14 percent of the variation in earnings from one company to another can be traced to differences in compensation practices.[14] Major investors such as the California Public Employee Retirement System (CalPERS) have begun to look at compensation in making investment decisions. Bob Boldt, CalPERS's senior investment manager for global public-company investments, wants to see a compensation system that helps employees think like owners. "We need a good mechanism to align the interests of CalPERS with the interests of Joe in engineering," he told a reporter.[15]

What's interesting about compensation is that it has progressed so far beyond the traditional equation of salary and benefits. Total compensation today can be highly variable, with substantial bonuses tied to individual performance, corporate performance, or both. Many employees—not just those of the defunct dot-coms—get stock options or outright share ownership through an employee stock-ownership plan (ESOP). According to the National Center for Employee Ownership in Oakland, California, some 4,000 companies in the United States with eight to ten million employees distribute stock options widely—that is, beyond the top management level. About 11,500 companies, with 8.5 million employees, have some form of ESOP or stock bonus plan.[16] Even closely held companies can (and many do) provide so-called phantom stock or earnings-based bonuses that tie long-term compensation to company performance.

As for benefits, the most important one today may be something that is less tangible than many: a family-friendly workplace. Johnson & Johnson lets workers bring children to work during the summer, where camps can pick them up and leave them off. Mattel Inc. shuts down Friday afternoons to let employees be with their kids.[17] In a landmark study sponsored by the Ford Foundation, researchers found that workplace planning based on employees' family needs can cut absenteeism by 30 percent and improve on-time project completion.[18]

Learning

Large companies in recent years have done plenty of classroom-based training. As noted above, it has almost certainly paid off in terms of financial performance. But astute companies know that classroom work is but a small part of the kind of training and development that adds to the stock of human capital. On an individual level, they expose young managers to a variety of jobs and locations, adding to their experience. They rotate line employees in and out of particular slots, broadening their skills. They also send them outside, to get a broad-based education. In a particularly dramatic demonstration of the value businesses are now placing on education, United Technologies Corp. operates one of the biggest college-scholarship programs anywhere. In 2000, according to the company, 13,349 UTC employees were paid to attend college. That brought the total spent by the company on college educations to $230.75 million over a five-year period, or 59 percent more than Yale University and Dartmouth College combined spent on scholarships over the same period. The program pays the entire cost of a college education for both full-time and part-time employees; even laid-off employees are eligible for up to a full year of schooling. Chairman and CEO George David launched the program because he wanted UTC to have "the best educated workforce on the planet."[19]

The newest developments in training and development are the various techniques companies have found to become what management theorist Peter Senge calls the "learning organization." For example:

Knowledge Management. The phrase has become a buzzword, to be sure, but some organizations are actually learning how to disseminate the information and know-how possessed by some employees to the organization as a whole. Siemens, for example—a "best practice" knowledge-management company in the eyes of the Houston-based American Productivity and Quality Center—has created an internal Web site called ShareNet, accessible by Siemens sales employees anywhere in the world. Part chat room, part database, part search engine, the site allows colleagues to enter information they think might be useful, and to search for advice on topics they need help on.

Launched in 1999 for $7.8 million, the tool has generated an estimated $122 million in sales. "In Switzerland, Siemens won a $460,000 contract to build a telecommunications network for two hospitals even though its bid was 30% higher than a competitor's," reported *BusinessWeek*. "The clincher: Via ShareNet, colleagues in the Netherlands provided technical data to help the sales rep prove that Siemens' system would be substantially more reliable."[20]

Social Capital.   If "knowledge management" is formal information-sharing, usually through a Web site or other database, "social capital" refers to informal information sharing, the kind that happens in hallway conversations or over a cup of coffee at a nearby diner. Companies can foster the development of social capital, argue researchers Laurence Prusak and Don Cohen, by creating space and time for get-togethers. Software company SAS offers a food plan, which encourages employees to get together over lunch. At the Steelcase Corporation headquarters employees have whiteboards outside their offices "to advertise what they're working on and invite comment." Companies can also discourage social capital by eliminating permanent office space or permitting too much "virtual" commuting.[21] The informally structured groups are a powerful form of social capital, and have been studied by Etienne Wenger and his colleagues and christened communities of practice. These groups—salespeople sharing information about their customers, repair technicians sharing their experience with different kinds of problems, and so on—can be powerful vehicles for improving everyone's skills. A "tech club" at DaimlerChrysler is an example: It includes engineers who work in different units but who get together regularly to talk about common concerns, such as brake design.[22]

Retention.   Retention is primarily a dependent variable. It depends not only on how a company handles other human-capital issues but on how it stacks up on the workplace-organization dimensions discussed in the next chapter. Even so, retention is critically important. Replacing people, particularly at higher levels, is costly and time-consuming. The training provided by a company, and the informal learning of its employees, means nothing unless people stay with the company. Given these costs alone, it's astonishing how many companies don't even track retention rates. Annual turnover is an intangible that, if nobody's watching it, can spiral out of control, with devastating effects on the bottom line.

There's another dimension of retention that bears watching as well: It reflects the day-in, day-out quality of a company's management. Researchers have found that, whatever the compensation and other benefits provided by a workplace, people will leave if they don't feel well treated by their immediate supervisors. The Gallup Organization's long-term study, mentioned earlier in this book, determined that employees' relationships with their immediate supervisors are more important than pay or perks in determining retention. Research by Dr. B. Lynn Ware and Bruce Fern, retention specialists with a California consulting firm, found that "the manager plays a significant role in influencing the employee's commitment level and retention."[23]

Following the finding that companies making Fortune's 1993 list of Most Admired Companies were more likely than others to utilize up-ward evaluation, 360-degree feedback, or other tools for assessing their managerial ranks, other Fortune 500 companies spent hundreds of millions of dollars over the subsequent years on such programs. However, many were met with disappointment in the results because too many organizations "adopt 360-degree feedback without clearly defining the mission and the scope of the program. Consequently, employees who receive the feedback are left to figure out for themselves how to cope with the results and tend not to develop goals and action plans following 360-degree applications."[24] In other words, simply putting a program in place without any increased attention paid to employee sentiments has limited if any value. Even with the economic downturn that started in early 2000, many companies still face a struggle for the loyalty of their employees. As Roxanna Frost, former Microsoft group program manager for executive management and development put it, "Let's be clear. We have a volunteer workforce."

Of course, one key to maximizing a company's human capital is to create an organization and a culture that get the best out of people. To this subject we now turn.

WORKPLACE ORGANIZATION AND CULTURE

It's the way the organization creates a meeting of minds among people. How do you send a very strong signal that this is a meritocracy, and this is a place where you are allowed to have a bit of fun, to think unlike the norm, where you are allowed to make a mistake?

—Jorma Ollila, Chairman and CEO,
Nokia Corporation[1]

More than two decades ago, a journalist and researcher named Robert Levering got a call from a publisher, who asked him if he'd be interested in writing a book called *The 100 Best Companies to Work for in America*. The publisher had a great title, he replied, but it would have to be a work of fiction. At that time in our economic history, Levering figured it would be easier to write a book called *The 100 Worst Companies to Work For*. The publisher said they didn't have enough lawyers on staff to let him write that book.

Nevertheless, Levering and colleague Milton Moskowitz agreed to write the "100 Best" book. It came out in 1984, and it was a sensation. "Thousands of managers and ordinary employees alike wanted to read about the unusual workplaces we had discovered," Levering remembers. "Several regional magazines copied the idea with magazine articles about the best employers in such cities as Atlanta, Seattle, and Dallas. Authors in Canada, Australia, and Holland wrote similar books in those countries." By the time the revised and updated edition of the book appeared, in 1993, the authors realized they had a tiger by the tail. Since then, the Great Place to Work Institute, co-founded by Levering and headquartered in San Francisco, has produced annual lists for a variety of publications around the world. Companies work hard to make the list—and when they do, they often trumpet the fact in full-page ads in the business press. "Companies all over the world," says Levering, "are competing with each other to become known as the best employer in their industry or community." [2]

The competition to make such lists—and the fact that Levering and his colleagues have found it easier and easier over time to find "great" workplaces—is a reflection of the Intangibles Economy. Many companies understand the point we made in the last chapter, namely, that their future depends on their ability to attract and retain good people, and above all to get them working together effectively. This last—the "working together" part—is the subject to which we now turn.

The High-Performance Workplace

Human beings are social animals, and any group of human beings—a workplace, say—is a social system. This is hardly an earth-shattering revelation, but many companies seem to ignore it. They spend money on the individual parts of human-resource management, such as recruitment and training, and forget about the social parts. The workplace often becomes like a dysfunctional family, a hotbed of office politics, a place where bright people seem to work very hard but nothing much gets done. Creativity- and innovation-killing phrases such as "put it in writing," "we've already tried that," and "don't rock the boat" are commonplace in organizations that have a distaste for experimentation and change. Companies characterized as great places to work, by contrast, are more like loving families. They're characterized by trust and mutual respect. People go out of their way to help one another, and politics takes a back seat. Indeed, employees at one of these workplaces often say, "It's like a family at work."

Like intangibles such as leadership, a productive workplace culture comes in many shapes and forms. There's no single recipe for creating one, any more than there's a single recipe for training effective leaders. Southwest Airlines is known for its zany, fun-loving workplace culture—one in which flight attendants have been known to sing the safety instructions and even to hide in the overhead luggage bins. Goldman Sachs, the blue-chip investment house, is known for its intense, goal-driven culture, in which people at all levels are expected to put aside personal objectives for the good of the firm. Both companies are leaders in their industries in part because of those cultures. Still, a substantial amount of research has been done on the subject of a productive workplace culture, usually under the rubric of what's called the high-performance workplace. The conclusions of researchers are remarkably similar. Though there's no recipe for creating a high-performance workplace, there are policies and practices that seem indispensable to it. We count four key elements; without a healthy dose of each one, a company is likely to run into a dead end.

Empowerment

It's interesting to go back eight or ten years and peruse the literature on the workplace. Business magazines wrote about frontline workers for Marriott hotels, who were no longer just doormen but "guest service associates" empowered to check in guests, pick up their keys and paperwork, and take them straight to their rooms. Professional journals, such as *Training*, were discovering that automobile assembly lines were no longer the grim repositories of routine work that they had once been. An article on Chrysler's Belvidere, Illinois, assembly plant, which was producing the Dodge Neon, reported that employees were shifting jobs, offering suggestions about how to improve things, planning their own training, and collaborating with the engineers on the very design of the line.[3] Newspapers ran reports as well. At steelmaker LTV, the *New York Times* reported, unionized production workers decided on new hires, made sales calls, visited customers to help resolve quality problems, and helped to select suppliers.[4] At global power company AES Corporation, said the *Wall Street Journal*, a team of blue-collar workers even took on the job of managing the plant's cash.[5] The idea was to devolve authority on front line employees: production operatives, salespeople, customer-service reps, service workers.

Academic research at the time bore out the effectiveness of such practices. A study of sixty-two auto-assembly plants around the world indicated that plants operating on this basis outperformed more traditional plants on both productivity and quality.[6] A study of steel-finishing lines determined that production lines with a full range of innovative workplace practices were about 7 percent more productive than those managed on a traditional basis.[7] A large study—examining a national sample of nearly 1,000 companies—determined that high-performance work practices led to lower turnover and higher sales, profits, and market value. The study also indicated that annual sales per employee can be as much as $100,000 higher in businesses with the "best" work practices than in firms with the "worst."[8]

C. K. Prahalad, a highly-influential professor and consultant, hailing from the University of Michigan, took a leave and began his own high-tech company, Praja, in April 2000. While still in the midst of the difficulties abundant in so many start-ups—the company is, as of this writing, still profitless and wrestling with layoffs—Prahalad is also struggling to put his long-espoused ideas about work into play. In fact, even the name *praja*, meaning "common people" in Sanskrit, speaks to the ends he is trying to achieve within his organization. Said Prahalad of his employee philosophy, "This company was started with the basic assumption that we would empower people to be themselves, to experience life on their terms." The challenge of allowing people to discover themselves, however, can prove elusive. Pralahad was surprised that his employees wanted clear role definition explained, and that they expressed anxiety that his emphasis on "constant learning" was causing the company to move too slowly. Still, Pralahad puts a lot of emphasis on empowering his employees and creating a team. "With wolves, solidarity is first. But when they hunt, they change roles. The implicit hierarchy depends on who does what."

Open Communication

A consistent finding in the Great Place to Work research is that the best workplaces are characterized by a high degree of trust. Management has credibility. So do line employees—if they say something needs to be fixed or a problem solved, management believes them. The way to establish such trust, of course, is to communicate, regularly and openly. Real communication is far different from the combination of newsletters, PR videos, and glitzy intranet sites that most large companies now employ. Some of it can be done through suggestion systems and e-mail. Most has to be done face to face, in regular meetings, so that people can ask questions. Good communication tells employees not only what management wants them to hear (and think), but what's really going on—the uncertainties as well as the done deals, the problems as well as the successes. Said Stuart Abraham, formerly director of systems integration at AT&T Laboratories: "An innovator takes pride in being outside the box, and in a large corporation the box is the way the corporation generally does business. So you need to know within what dimensions you can be outside the box and within what dimensions, to be maximally effective, you need to align [with] where the corporation is going."

The system known as "open-book management" takes communication to its logical conclusion. Open-book companies make a point of telling employees the real numbers—business-unit financial results, costs, budgets, performance targets, and so on—that managers are using to run the business. For instance, at Steel Dynamics, an American minimill company that grew to $700 million revenues in only seven years of operation, employees know the cost of virtually everything—including the $10 probes utilized to test the temperature of the furnace. "The guy who sticks the probe into the furnace . . . is going to want to do that only once, not four times," says the mill's manager.[9] Pay incentives tied to cost savings encourage the workers to pay close attention to such matters.

The company with the most experience in open-book management is probably SRC Holdings Corporation, in Springfield, Missouri. Originally known as Springfield ReManufacturing Corporation, SRC was once a struggling spinoff from International Harvester (now Navistar) that did little more than rebuild diesel engines. Today it is a twenty-two-company miniconglomerate with several manufacturing and business-service enterprises, nearly all of which operate on open-book principles. One key to the systems' success is both the depth and breadth of communication about business matters:

> The highlight of any SRC plant tour, whether blue-collar or white-collar, is the array of measurement-rich wall charts. For example, at Megavolt, [a] joint venture with CNH Global that produces electrical equipment, a green posterboard shows plantwide efficiency, and a red posterboard shows how much of the finished product was secondhand [the more used parts instead of new parts, the greater the savings]. There's also a cafeteria with two fair-sized walls covered with charts that show, among other things, all the income and expense breakdowns for the past month. . . . Since the charts get updated daily, people know very early whether they will hit their monthly targets and why. "That's the key," [general manager Dianna] Devore said. "If a plan projected $332 in overtime and we're paying out $351 halfway through, we know that we must react. Something is happening. If we waited for an accounting person to tell us [the numbers], it would be too late to do anything about it.[10]

When communication breaks down in organizations, relationships are damaged, sometimes beyond repair. And the function of good communication cannot be underestimated, so much so that a new generation of management consultants are becoming much more commonplace in organizations. In November 2001, the *Wall Street Journal* wrote about the trend of consulting psychotherapists' becoming more a part of corporate cultures.[11] These consultants focus on workplace breakdowns, such as emotional barriers, where open communication is not practiced. These psychotherapists specialize at helping employees understand communication problems and come up with constructive ways to improve them.

Performance Measurement

In 1994, Gordon Bethune took over as CEO of Continental Airlines. The company had been struggling, and was notorious for poor customer service. In particular, its on-time performance placed it among the worst of U.S. airlines. Bethune decided to post Continental's on-time performance each month, and to give every employee a small bonus—$65—if it was in the top five. Three months later it ranked first. In 2000 it ranked first for the entire year, with an on-time rating 5.5 percentage points higher than the industry average.

"What gets measured gets done." The business cliché is accurate as far as it goes, but it doesn't go very far. The fact is, performance measurement is a difficult tool to implement effectively. On the one hand, there can be no high-performance workplace without it. All the empowerment and communication are no more than nice things to do unless they translate into better performance, and better performance isn't known until it is measured in some way. On the other hand, measurement can be wrongheaded, demoralizing, or simply irrelevant. Three guidelines are:

Measure a variety of objectives—in reality as well as theory.   The story is told of the fast-food chain that supposedly tracked a variety of metrics, but, in reality, what senior managers paid attention to most was the amount of cooked chicken that was thrown away. (This was known as "chicken efficiency.") The result? Restaurant managers didn't cook chicken until somebody ordered it. Customers might wait twenty minutes for their meal, but at least the managers weren't throwing away too much chicken![12] In Continental's case, a single-minded focus on on-time departures could have alienated passengers if gate attendants were hurried or rude, let alone if mechanics cut corners on maintenance. In fact Continental was able to pull off an improvement on one key metric without sacrificing others.

Measure intangibles as well as tangibles. Marketing departments can track customer satisfaction and other measures of brand equity. HR units can measure their success at recruitment and retention. Some performance objectives, such as on-time departure for an airline, are key elements of business success and need to be tracked independently. (The importance of intangibles is that they are often leading indicators—more effective at forecasting market direction—whereas financials let you know what has already happened.) Thus customer-satisfaction rates or the number of products in the R&D pipeline are likely to be leading indicators of revenues tomorrow.

Involve employees in setting goals. Need it be said? Performance measurement can be both carrot and stick. The "stick" part doesn't work well over time; indeed, there's a long history in business of workers learning to beat the "rate"—the expected level of performance for a given wage—and then seeing the rate increased. If employees are involved in setting their own targets, ironically, they'll often set the bar higher than management would. If they're appropriately rewarded for meeting or beating the goals, the measurements will feel more like keeping score and less like a managerial report card.

Passion and Commitment

You find these intangibles in strange places. Southwest Airlines and Goldman Sachs, mentioned earlier, are hotbeds of passion and commitment, partly because they both devote enormous amounts of time and effort to hiring people that they think will fit well with their cultures. Start-ups are known for the passion and commitment they engender— including some start-ups that are divisions of large companies.

Then again, some companies—notably several of those that make the Great Places to Work list—seem to engender passion and commitment in other ways. Take the Container Store, for example, a U.S. chain that expected to do roughly $260 million in revenues for 2001. The Container Store was ranked number one on the Great Places list for both 2000 and 2001; it won *Workforce* magazine's 2001 award for outstanding people-management strategies. The in-house culture— bolstered, as at Southwest and Goldman, by careful attention to hiring—is egalitarian and open. Managers work alongside employees, and employees help each other. ("I've worked at companies where the boss sits behind a desk and says, 'Do this, do that,'" said one twenty-year-old, "and I'm like, 'You do it.' Here everyone does everything. It's like a team.") Full financials are open for all to see. People learn central values, such as cultivating an "air of excitement," and repeat them to one another. Employees make between two and three times the industry average, and even part-timers get full benefits. Everyone receives a whopping 235 hours of training in their first year, and 160 hours a year thereafter. An astonishing fraction—97 percent—of employees agree with the survey statement, "People care about each other here."

The result: Turnover is about one-third of the industry average for salespeople, and about one-sixth of the industry average for managers. "A funny thing happens when you take the time to educate your employees, pay them well, and treat them as equals," said president Kip Tindell. "You end up with extremely motivated and enthusiastic people."[13]

Like the other intangibles in these chapters, the high-performance workplace is a cluster of attributes, some easier to define than others. The basic checklist includes opportunities for skills enhancement and information sharing; employee participation in decision-making; a de-layered organizational structure that includes cross-functional teams and other means for sharing innovative ideas; compensation linked to performance and skills; employment security rather than job security, meaning that employees receive training to upgrade their skills and adequate support should layoffs become unavoidable; recognition that the union (if the organization is unionized) is a partner rather than an adversary; a supportive work environment; employee involvement in the evaluation and purchase of new technologies; and the meshing of human, organizational, and intellectual resource practices with other business strategies.[14]

These factors emerged directly from the experience of managers who were groping for answers to the problems they faced as global competition grew ever more cutthroat. They were practical responses that worked in some combination—often different from one organization to another—and that were then validated by academic research and experience elsewhere.

"Soft stuff." "Squishy." These are issues that managers used to be too embarrassed to talk about if they cared to be promoted. Suddenly, the so-called hard numbers are being restated and all those soft, non-financial—but quantifiable—cultural factors are being blamed for failed acquisitions or lauded as the source of future growth and profits.

INNOVATION

There are very tough economic conditions out there. And most of our industry is retrenching. We decided to find a different path to navigate through this difficult economic time. Our path is innovation.

—Steve Jobs, Cofounder and CEO, Apple Corporation; Chairman and CEO, Pixar

Innovation has always been a key to business success and wealth creation. It has always been a central driver of economic development. But when people say "innovation" they usually mean some new invention, like the Walkman or the digital camera. As important as such products may be, to limit the discussion of innovation to new inventions or technologies is rather like limiting a discussion of marketing to the latest ad campaigns. It's only the tip of a rather large iceberg.

In fact, a hallmark of the Intangibles Economy is that product innovation is no longer sufficient to stay in the competitive race. Rather, companies must innovate across a variety of fronts:

SERVICE INNOVATION

"Inventions" usually refer to new products—but what about whole new services? Twenty years ago Merrill Lynch pioneered the so-called Cash Management Account, which since then has been widely copied by other investment houses. Business checking accounts weren't allowed to receive interest. Companies were spending long hours trying to keep enough cash in their checking accounts to pay their bills, while maximizing interest income by keeping the rest in a money-market fund. Merrill combined a money fund with a checking account, in effect turning itself into something like a bank. Today, financial companies compete to offer consumers a variety of sophisticated services. Fidelity Investments and GMAC, for instance, have teamed up to let well-heeled customers obtain a low-cost mortgage (for themselves or family members) simply by pledging a certain amount of assets held in a Fidelity account.

BUSINESS MODEL INNOVATION

Think of Amazon.com and its many emulators, which have created virtual stores. Think of Dell Computer, which constructed an entire supply chain around build-to-order manufacturing (and is now being studied by other manufacturers from auto companies to appliance producers). In retail, "category-killer" stores, such as Home Depot and Staples, are by now an old innovation, though one that continues to be successful. In a newer variant, furniture retailer Ikea succeeds by focusing on a combination of innovative design and low cost. Its assemble-it-yourself design takes some 40 percent of the cost out of the average item sold in its stores. In computer software, companies such as Red Hat take a product that is essentially free—the Linux operating system—and combine it with services and support to create a marketable package.

ORGANIZATIONAL INNOVATION

Visa International has been called an "inverted holding company," an organization that is owned by the banks it serves. The structure of the organization reflects this: It's a federal system, with regional, national, and international organizations each drawing power from the levels below (instead of the levels above). Member banks stay in only if the organization works for them; they are "free to use any Visa product, to leave the whole Visa organization if they choose, and to offer competing products. (In fact, most banks offer the primary competing product, Mastercard.)"[1] Another innovative organization of recent times: the so-called reverse franchise, such as Century 21 Real Estate, in which existing businesses affiliate with a national organization for marketing purposes.

INTERNAL-PROCESS INNOVATION

In the past, Boeing Co. designed its airplanes using computer-aided engineering drawings. Each new plane involved 100,000 or more designed parts; when any two of them interfered with one another, the design had to be modified. With the 777, however, Boeing created a system it dubbed EPIC, for Electronic Preassembly in the Computer. The new system allowed engineers to design their parts and systems electronically and check the design with other engineers before anything was built.[2] But Boeing isn't relying exclusively on high-tech innovations. The company's so-called Moonshine Shops, or skunk works—charged with reducing manufacturing time and costs—have come up with a wide variety of low-tech process changes, such as using a hay loader rather than a costly overhead crane to get passenger seats in the door of a plane under construction. Thanks to such innovations, the time required to assemble major components into a completed airplane has fallen from 71 days in late 1998 to 37, and gross margins have risen accordingly.[3]

"PROFIT-ZONE" INNOVATION

It used to be that manufacturers made things, distribution companies distributed them, and service companies provided service. But not all the points in the value chain are equally profitable, and in the so-called New Economy, companies are migrating their businesses to higher-margin operations. Lou Gerstner has revived IBM mainly by moving it heavily into the provision of computer services rather than manufacturing. Emerson Electric—the largest U.S. maker of compressors for refrigeration, heating, and air-conditioning systems— used the Internet a few years ago to begin offering a new service business: monitoring these systems remotely. When the company's systems detected fluctuations in the power flowing to an Atlanta supermarket, threatening to shut down the store's mechanical systems, an Emerson employee quickly notified a store manager, who dispatched an engineer to fix the problem. "They would have lost $100,000 in that store in fresh foods if the refrigeration system had failed," said Charles Peters, a senior executive VP and e-business leader at Emerson.[4]

ALLIANCE INNOVATION

Pharmaceutical companies excel at what might be called traditional innovation, namely, the development and introduction of new drugs. In recent years they have developed software that helps them to identify successful new compounds much faster than in the past, and they have created alliances with biotech companies, who serve as a kind of leading-edge research-and-development lab for their larger partners (see chapter ten). But their innovation doesn't stop there: Unlike in the past, they have built alliances with a variety of outsourcing partners. Specialized manufacturing firms provide everything from specific chemicals to packaged finished goods. Contract-research organizations manage clinical trials and bring drugs to market. Consulting firm Arthur D. Little says that pharmaceutical outsourcing in the United States is now a $30-billion business.[5] Other good examples of the alliance phenomena include airlines, with their code-sharing and frequent-flyer program combinations, and entertainment companies, who may simultaneously be each other's fiercest competitors, major suppliers, and most important customers thanks to the interlocking web of music, film, broadcast, cable, and publishing interests.

MARKETING INNOVATION

Harrah's, which began in the late 1930s as a bingo parlor in Reno, Nevada, has since grown to become the largest casino entertainment company in North America. The company's most notable expansion decision did not involve building and acquiring more hotels and casinos—although it did do that—nor did it simply acquire new types of slot machines. Rather, in 1997, Harrah's launched Total Rewards, the gaming industry's first national player-rewards program, connecting customers' activity throughout all the company's Harrah's-brand venues. Similar to an airline frequent-flyer program, points are earned by customers when they play, which can then be redeemed for cash, merchandise, food, lodging, or show tickets at any Harrah's facility. The program encourages guests to gamble at more than twenty-one Harrah's casinos, but more important, the vast body of personal information Harrah's gathers about its customers enables the casino to market to the individual preferences of the respective venue's clientele. This increases the customers' satisfaction and reduces the demand volatility at its venues, with all of the ancillary benefits to expense management and cost of capital that implies. This is made possible by an emphasis on information technology (interestingly, Harrah's was named number two in *Computerworld*'s 1999 list of Top 100 Best Places to Work in IT) that has permitted the company to assemble a database of more than 19 million customers, the data from which can itself be sold to other businesses as appropriate opportunities allow. "We have a P&L on each customer," says senior vice president of brand operations and information technology, John Boushy. "That has been fundamental for us in learning which marketing program has the greatest impact and value to the customers as measured by their behavior."[6]

STRATEGIC INNOVATION

Only a few years ago, America Online was a struggling Internet service provider. Today it sits atop a merger with the giant Time Warner entertainment and publishing empire. Who would have thought it possible? As it happened, AOL's 1999 decision to buy Time Warner was excoriated by those who believed that the "new paradigm" Internet companies would simply destroy old-economy dinosaurs such as the publishing and entertainment giant. But the merger provided AOL with a host of tangible and intangible benefits, including earnings stability, new channels, marketing synergies, and creative talent. When the downturn hit, it was AOL Time Warner whose stock price and stability kept it from suffering the fate of many erstwhile competitors.

Of course, more traditional kinds of innovation—new technologies, new products—have flowered in today's economy as well. Napster invented a system of file sharing that capitalized on all the unused memory in computers that are hooked up to the Internet; though Napster's application itself was declared illegal, there is no doubt that so-called peer-to-peer networking will have many legal applications in the future. DaimlerChrysler learned how to use what is known as "3D stereo lithography" to create digital and then plastic life-size models of car parts, cutting prototype-design time significantly. In one fascinating application of high technology to a low-tech product, Arena North America developed a competition swimsuit with tiny, almost imperceptible V-shaped and angled grooves. Based on NASA research on how to prevent the so-called turbulence bursts of aerodynamics and hydrodynamics, the suit can reduce flow-friction rates by as much as 10 percent.[7]

The list could go on, but the point seems indisputable: The Intangibles Economy encourages, thrives on, and, in fact, requires companies to be innovative along many dimensions.

MANAGING FOR SUCCESSFUL INNOVATION

As this brief review suggests, managing innovation in today's economy is all about managing intangibles. There are four imperatives:

Leadership: Make Resources Available

In summer 2000, Eli Lilly was in trouble. The term of patent protection for Prozac, its blockbuster antidepression drug, had been challenged in court, and Lilly had lost; according to the judge's ruling, Prozac would come off patent in a year rather than in three years, as Lilly had hoped. The company's stock plunged, wiping out $36.8 billion in market cap. Twelve months later, generic pharmaceutical maker Barr Laboratories entered the market with its version of the chemical in Prozac, at a price 20 percent to 40 percent less than the original. Lilly expected to lose some $2.4 billion in annual sales, nearly a quarter of its total revenue. "As CEO Sidney Taurel often points out," read one report, "no company has survived a patent expiration of this magnitude without losing its independence."[8]

Taurel, however, had done just what a leader in this economy has to do: poured resources into innovation. He increased the R&D budget by 30 percent, brought on 700 new scientists, and ordered the company's researchers to focus on drugs capable of producing more than $500 million in revenue. The result: "Lilly now has a medicine cabinet stocked full of promising new drugs, including treatments for schizophrenia and for sepsis. . . . Provided that management is able to handle some significant challenges from regulators and competitors, those new products could more than offset Prozac's loss in just 12 months."[9] Lilly shares had partially rebounded by autumn 2001. Its market-to-book ratio by then was higher than the pharmaceutical industry average and considerably higher than the S&P 500 average.

Strategy Execution: Deliver on Your Innovative Promises

Innovation is such a hot commodity in today's economy that companies are tempted to overpromise. Software firms are notorious for announcing "vaporware"—programs that are nowhere near ready for market—in hopes of discouraging competitors. New companies routinely promise the sky—and as the dot-coms showed, the sky is likely to fall in on them. But even well-respected businesses such as Palm Inc. can run into trouble from an inability to deliver an innovation.

Palm's troubles began with the economic downturn of 2001. Sales of its handheld computers were off, and the company wanted to announce an innovative new product right away in hopes of adding to its revenues. Managers promised senior executives that the product would be ready to go in two weeks. Palm made the announcement, but in fact it would be six weeks before the new devices—the so-called m500 line—were ready to ship in volume. Meanwhile, consumers decided to hold off on buying older Palm products. Sales slumped. So did Palm's stock, which at one point was down 95 percent over a ten-month period. What happened? Poor execution, pure and simple. Preoccupied with a new headquarters building, senior execs were paying little attention to operations. A key operations-management job went unfilled. There wasn't enough time for testing the new models, so the manufacturing subcontractor ran into both design and performance problems. (In one model, the battery didn't fit.) Eventually Palm had to lay off hundreds of people—and stop construction on that new headquarters.[10]

Processes: Encourage Bottom-Up Innovation, or "Intrapreneur-ship"

No leader can do everything that needs to be done, because ideas about new products or production methods often must come from others in the organization. The question is whether a company stimulates or discourages the creation and testing of new ideas. At the level of workplace processes, the kind of empowerment described in the previous chapter is a requirement, along with a workplace culture that encourages and rewards suggestions for improvements. Companies can also stimulate the development of new products and business units. The 3M Corporation is legendary for doing so; others have learned in the past few years. Thus Royal Dutch Shell's exploration and production division went so far as to set up an internal "venture board" to review new ideas and business plans created by division employees. Siemens's Strategic Business Development Group sponsors business-plan competitions.[11]

One key to success in all such enterprises is to realize that many— perhaps most—new ideas may be wrongheaded, and that even seemingly promising ones may wind up in failure. Strategy consultant Gary Hamel made the point with his usual flair for colorful language:

> In devoting themselves entirely to the pursuit of efficiency, top management inadvertently drives out the "waste" and "extravagance" that is the very fuel of innovation. As top management strives for ever greater efficiency, it must learn to tolerate "stupid" ideas and "failed" experiments. After all, when a man and a woman celebrate conception, they seldom bemoan the 59 million little swimmers that never made it.[12]

Brand: Manage for Innovation

Marketers long ago learned to manage line extensions, such as Bud Light and Crest mint gel, although exactly how far a line can productively be extended is always a matter of debate. But innovation of the kind required in today's economy adds a whole new dimension to brand management. What happens to a retailer's brand, for example, when the company puts some or all of its wares online? The customer is no longer subject to the same kind of in-store merchandising, can no longer be wooed by professional salespeople, can no longer touch and feel the goods. So protecting the brand in this kind of innovation requires paying attention to a whole new kind of marketing. How is the site presented? What goods are sold on it? What kinds of customer service and back-office support are available? The answers will differ from one retailer to another, but none can afford to ignore the opportunities and constraints presented by its brand.

The issues are even greater when a company branches beyond into new business arenas. IBM has famously recreated itself as a service company; its brand was strong enough to support the new emphasis on delivering solutions to customers, as opposed to simply delivering hardware. Had Hewlett-Packard succeeded in buying the consulting division of PricewaterhouseCoopers (which it tried to do before acquiring Compaq Computer), the prospects would have been much less clear. Is the H-P name—so well known in one arena—extendable into the wholly different arena of management consulting? What has made Virgin so successful in extending its brand (see chapter eight) is the fact that the name stands for something—a style, a culture—that transcends any particular business. It's not clear that the famous "H-P way" is anything comparable.

This list could go on, but we hope we have made our point. Nowhere, perhaps, is the interaction between one intangible and others so clear as it is in respect to innovation. An innovative company—an effective one—almost by definition is a company that manages its other intangibles well.

INTELLECTUAL CAPITAL

An ever-increasing share of GDP has reflected the value of ideas more than material substance or manual labor input.

—Alan Greenspan, Chairman,
U.S. Federal Reserve System

Intellectual capital refers to the value of ideas. If the economic history of the last half-century is about the transition from industrial might to service and then to knowledge as the driving force of the economy, intellectual capital is the currency that has fueled that evolution. "The key assets of corporations are no longer natural resources, machinery or even financial capital, but intangibles—R&D and proprietary know-how, intellectual property, workforce skills, world-class supply networks and brands," declared a High Level Expert Group empaneled in 2000 by the European Commission. "Far from being new topics, knowledge and intangibles have been important throughout history. The difference is that today, a firm's intangible assets are often the key element in its competitiveness. Increasingly, the capacity to combine external and internal sources of knowledge to exploit commercial opportunities has become a distinctive competency."[1]

Alan Greenspan would agree. So would any number of other experts. So, indeed, would the average newspaper reader perusing stories such as these:

- General Motors sues former purchasing executive Jose Ignacio (Inaki) Lopez when he leaves to join Volkswagen. The charge is that he has stolen GM secrets and given them to a competitor.
- Disney and other film companies enhance the value of their increasingly expensive and risky offerings by signing licensing deals that turn movie characters into children's toys, books, games, and TV shows.
- Airlines buy and sell "assets" such as landing slots and access to airport gates.
- Business processes, from simple equipment-operating tips to complex supply-chain-management strategies, sometimes exceed the value of the machines and material they are designed to control.
- Exchanges and corporate entities begin making markets (offering to buy and sell) in a variety of securities or securitized commodities, such as metals, forest products, bandwidth, pollution credits, and weather derivatives; various governments hold successful auctions of telecommunications bandwidth.
- The Patent & License Exchange (pl-x), Aurigin, and other companies are created with the express purpose of making markets in intellectual capital. In 2001, pl-x claimed to value and manage more than $90 billion in notional intellectual-property value.
- A 1996 study commissioned by the International Intellectual Property Alliance estimated that the U.S. creative industries—computer software, music, film, and publishing—contributed almost $280 billion to the Gross Domestic Product, and accounted for some 3.5 million jobs, surpassing any single manufacturing sector by both measures. The estimated $60 billion of foreign sales and

exports by these industries in 1996 made them the leading export sector of the entire economy.[2]

- Former President Bill Clinton signed a deal in 2001 to write his memoirs for $10 million, exceeding the $8-million deal offered his wife a year earlier (and the $7.1 million paid to former GE chief executive Jack Welch).

- Perhaps no issue better captures the complexities of this change than the now infamous story of a company named Napster.

In the past, it wasn't hard to share files over networked computers, so long as you knew what you were doing—and so long as you knew who had the file you wanted. Academics could share research data; hackers could trade games. Shawn Fanning, the nineteen-year-old who dropped out of college to create Napster in 1999, came up with only a couple of new wrinkles. He created an easy-to-use interface that took the complexity out of file sharing. He also created a search engine that could find the file a user was looking for on somebody else's computer. Suddenly, computer users with the right equipment could download music over the Internet for free, just by connecting to Napster and searching for the songs they wanted. Suddenly, too, the $15-billion-a-year recording industry found its core assets available without cost to almost anyone who wanted them. A grandmother in England could download a song from a teenager in Taiwan without a penny changing hands.

The effects of this innovation were dramatic. In the first three months of 2001, approximately 2.5 billion files a month were being downloaded via Napster. In a typical story, the University of Indiana announced that it had to shut down its computer network and then prohibit Napster access—not because the university was morally or legally opposed to the company but because all the music fans in the student body had so overloaded the computer system that it could no longer function. From the fourth quarter of 2000 to the first quarter of 2001, net music shipments in the United States declined from over $8 billion to under $6 billion.

Then the Recording Industry Association of America's suit to shut down Napster was resolved in the RIAA's favor, and everyone in the music business breathed a deep sigh of relief. But the fact remains: Napster was probably just the proverbial camel's nose under the tent. So-called peer-to-peer (P2P) computing, of which Napster was an example, is seen by many as the next big wave of networking. "Gnutella, Mojo Nation, Lightshare, iMesh, and a host of other services are emerging to take peer-to-peer file sharing to the next level—commercialization—even as Napster-inspired underground utilities like Yo!NK and Konspire are eagerly passed around the Net," declared one report in early 2001.[3] Though some of the names will undoubtedly have changed by the time this book is published, the experiments are unlikely to have disappeared. Though Napster was designed for sharing only one type of files—so-called MP3 music files—sites such as Gnutella and Konspire enable users to share any type of file. Meanwhile, the Groove platform developed by Ray Ozzie (of Lotus Notes fame) aims to let corporations use P2P networks to improve customer service and supply-chain performance by, in the first case, connecting customers with other customers for the answer they seek. In the case of supply-chain management, these applications enable different parts of the chain to talk with each other rather than having to connect through a centralized data center. This speeds up the process and may lead to better solutions by encouraging operating units to communicate about their issues of immediate concern. Large companies such as Hewlett-Packard and Intel have formed a Peer-to-Peer Working Group designed to tackle security, bandwidth, interoperability, and other development issues in the belief that P2P, through its harnessing of disparate and informally connected sources, will provide the applications necessary to spark the next big run-up in technology use.

In effect, P2P allows intellectual capital of all sorts to zip untrammeled across the wires and waves of the Internet—a dramatic illustration of exactly how valuable intellectual capital can be, and how difficult it is for the creator or owner to capture that value.

THE IC MARKETPLACE

A world in which intellectual capital creates and defines so much economic value presents managers with several distinct sets of challenges. These challenges stem directly from the rules that govern markets in intellectual capital.

Intellectual property is created, typically, when someone invests a substantial amount of time and resources. It costs millions to make a feature-length movie, an elaborate piece of software, or an effective new pharmaceutical. Once it is developed, however, the intellectual property costs little or nothing to replicate and distribute. What's more, the value of any given copy may actually increase the more people use it. A book or movie that's being talked about—or a drug or piece of software that becomes the de facto standard—actually increases in value with time. And once the costs of development are recouped, as Microsoft chairman Bill Gates told an audience of CEOs not long ago, "every single additional unit is pure profit."[4]

Of course, there are two corresponding downsides. A piece of intellectual property that somehow doesn't live up to expectations—a drug that doesn't work, a movie that bombs—can produce huge losses, for all those expenditures on investment are lost forever. And even a successful piece of intellectual property is likely to have a limited shelf life. Drugs and software are made obsolete by better-performing competitors. Books and movies get old, and are replaced by newer ones.

Incidentally, we have been using the conventional examples of intellectual property—movies, software, drugs, printed matter—in the discussion so far. But one characteristic of our economy is that more and more conventional products and services incorporate high levels of in-tellectual capital, and the markets for them share some of these same attributes. A new microchip or high-performance router is valuable pri-marily because of its intellectual content, not because of the materials in it. A cable television network has greater or lesser value depending on the content it can deliver, on the number of subscribers it attracts, and on their loyalty to it rather than to competing technologies such as direct broadcast by satellite. Environmental issues have also taken a prominent role in this debate. Investment firms are marketing so-called green funds to college endowments and interested high-net-worth in-dividuals. These funds invest only in companies that pass certain kinds of screens indicating the company's commitment to sustainable growth or environmentally friendly stewardship. In 1999, socially responsible investing surpassed the $2 trillion mark in the United States, account-ing for one in every eight dollars under professional management.[5] Said former World Bank vice president Ismail Serageldin: "In an era in which natural capital was considered infinite relative to the scale of hu-man use, it was reasonable not to deduct natural capital from gross re-ceipts in calculating income. That era is now past."

At any rate, the markets for intellectual property raise several press-ing issues:

The Pressure Toward Monopoly

"In these industries," writes *Wall Street Journal* columnist Alan Murray, "there is no Avis"—that is, there's no number two.[6] Why should any-body use a competing word-processing program when virtually every office and publication now uses Microsoft Word? Why should any physician prescribe (or any patient accept) a drug that is slightly less effective than the standard treatment? In the real world, of course, there are nearly always competitors of some sort—not everybody uses MS-DOS computers—but in markets dominated by intellectual capi-tal the pressure is constantly toward the elimination of the also-rans in favor of the market leader.

This is true even for a service such as cable TV. In principle, it's possible to imagine a municipality allowing many competing cable systems (indeed, some municipalities do allow at least two). But if one of them is only slightly better, or offers the same quality at less cost, there's little reason for number two to exist—and all that investment is wasted. Recognizing this fact, most municipalities have chosen to treat cable as a natural monopoly and grant a franchise to only one company. Similarly, drug companies fight tooth and nail to maintain and extend the patent protection granted their brand-name drugs, in effect extending the temporary legal monopoly they have been granted by the patent system. Says Murray: "The only way to make money is to have monopoly power."

Valuation

How much is an investment in intellectual capital worth? And, by extension, what should be the value of a company that trades primarily on its intellectual capital? Talk about difficult calculations! Conventional accounting provides little guidance. The market is prone to overreact in one direction or another. The collapse of the dot-com companies and related Internet and technology stocks in 2001 can be attributed, in part, to massive overvaluation of difficult-to-value assets. Investors were told that history was no guide, and that if they questioned the "new" economy they just weren't "getting it." Yet when the collapse came, the intellectual capital that had once looked so valuable suddenly plunged to zero or near-zero.

Managers in companies that rely on intellectual capital face a similar dilemma every day. How much is a half-developed piece of software worth? Will a new technological improvement pay a return, or will it be made obsolete before, or soon after, it is brought to market? In effect, business executives must become risk managers, and learn the arts of placing and hedging bets. The good news is that market demand has spawned a variety of methods and programs to value what was once unable to be calculated. Some methods are for CFOs, some are for bank lending officers, some are for venture capitalists, and some are for general use. Whatever their flaws or benefits, their creation is a testament to the vibrancy of the market for this sort of service.

Regulation

The importance of intellectual capital as a national policy matter was signaled by the passage in the United States of the controversial Digital Millennium Copyright Act of 1998. In effect, this act recognized the importance of intellectual capital to business growth and profitability. It extended the protections already afforded so that companies forced by the nature of their business to make increasingly large up-front investments could recoup those investments at a "reasonable" rate. But opponents to the act claimed that the intellectual property rights of those protected were accorded greater value than were the rights of entrepreneurs and upstarts who were challenging marketplace incumbents. Obviously, this is a debate of which we haven't heard the end. The government's attitude toward the alleged monopolies created by Microsoft—first an aggressive antitrust prosecution, later a pullback that seemed to favor the company—reflects society's ambivalence.

As for accounting rules, the U.S. Financial Accounting Standards Board (FASB) did away with the pooling-of-interests accounting method by which many high-growth companies in the technology industry accounted for their acquisitions. This method permitted the treatment of "goodwill"—the excess of purchase price over the fair value of an acquired company—to be handled in such a way that it would not require a charge against earnings for amortization. Although pushed into compromise by those who had profited so enormously from this method, the FASB at least crafted a solution that forced companies to begin to recognize the actual market value of the businesses they acquired. This addressed the issue of intellectual capital valued too highly in theory to be valued fairly—eventually—in practice.

The International Accounting Standards Board (IASB) has also begun looking into the policy implications of intangibles disclosure.

Internal Management of Intellectual Capital

Intellectual capital isn't incorporated only into products and services sold on the marketplace; it's also incorporated in a company's internal business processes. The key to the quality movement, for example, was information—information that was meticulously and repetitively recorded, then acted upon. That was followed by the widespread interest in knowledge management (KM). Companies pursuing KM began systematically capturing the operational lore of the organization in written or verbal form, on a variety of media, then categorizing and organizing it. The goal was that everyone working on similar problems or opportunities in a large, complex, and dispersed enterprise should have access to the experience and knowledge of their colleagues. KM became increasingly important as corporations embraced the Schumpeterian concept of economic "gales of creative destruction"—a philosophical way of expressing the realpolitik of the millennial enterprise, namely that nothing was permanent—neither strategies, nor companies, nor the jobs that went with them. KM became a way of codifying the knowledge and experience of those whose employment might later be sacrificed to the "greater good."

The next phase of this internal intellectual-capital evolution was driven by advances in computerization. Data storage led to data mining, the employment of mathematical algorithms to glean useful information from huge databases. Using the techniques of data mining, companies could analyze and recombine information so that disparate bits of knowledge about habits and preferences could be assembled into patterns, then compared with information about target products. This, in turn, allowed the companies to craft more effective sales pitches. Companies such as Capital One Financial were created specifically to employ such tools. Cap One became the largest direct-mail marketer of financial services products through the adroit use of these advances.

MANAGING INTELLECTUAL CAPITAL

The first step for most corporate leadership teams is to acknowledge that their company does indeed have intellectual capital, and that this capital is of value to the enterprise. This is rarely as easy as it sounds. Executives must confront the truth—often uncomfortable—that how the organization actually creates value may be different from the notion they carry in their heads ("we drill for oil," "we make cars," or whatever). They also must realize that how the organization creates value is probably changing, and in all likelihood will continue to change. The continuing evolution of successful companies such as Citigroup, Enron, and General Electric underscores the importance—and value—of continually challenging traditional internal assumptions about products, brands, organizational structures, and business models. Our experience has convinced us that intellectual capital invariably contributes more to the company's value than its managers think. As you will see in the next section of the book, our research suggests that at least 50 percent of the market value of many traditional companies can be ascribed to such intangibles.

The second step is to determine which ideas matter and how much they matter. We have provided some approaches to answering these questions in the "Measures That Matter" and "IPO Success Factors" research described in chapters three and four. General propositions aside, in our experience it's always best to start within your own organization. Your colleagues and you know the company best. Surveying employees to establish a baseline about which ideas drive your business is the most useful first step. The advice of customers, suppliers, investors, and lenders, accessible through informal canvasing or formal surveys, also provide useful insights. Much has been written on the diverse managerial styles of organizations and the individuals within them; keep that in mind as you make your choices. As an intermediate "gut check," benchmarking against companies in your industry through your industry association, or against those whose management and operations you respect or against others that have launched intellectual capital initiatives of their own is an effective way of determining whether you are taking a direction that will lead to improved performance.

There is no final step in this process. We live in an era defined by volatility and uncertainty. Businesses have begun to shed their historical identities the way snakes shed their skins. It is a matter of survival. To be truly effective, evolutionary learning fed by constant experimentation is the only way to keep your evaluations relevant as your business and the economy around you change. The intellectual capital that matters to your business today may be irrelevant tomorrow. Investing only in one set of ideas is a ticket to organizational oblivion. Investing in a process that evaluates and identifies good ideas is the organizational equivalent of a biological imperative.

ADAPTABILITY

You better develop a team, and the team better be flexible on how there's money to be made. The ability to adapt is the focus and foundation of the new business plans that work with copyrights and content in this century.

—Chuck D., rap music artist
and entrepreneur

Funny thing about the course of business. Management theorists and practicing executives of the twentieth century devoted themselves to imagining and building the ideal hierarchical organization, the smoothly functioning company in which orders flowed from the top and were carried out by the lower ranks. Their counterparts in the twenty-first century will likely devote themselves to tearing this model down.

And what will replace it? A less hierarchical organization, certainly. A networked organization, in which information flows up, down, and sideways, all the time. An organization oriented toward process as well as product, teams as well as individuals, learning as well as doing. An organization that can adapt to changing conditions—that can turn on a dime (or a franc or a yen). Such companies will be fast, flexible, and focused on their core competencies. Their managers will be coaches, their knowledge workers empowered to reengineer and continuously improve their processes.

This is an appealing vision, and every forward-thinking manager you care to talk to would probably endorse it in one form or another. Trouble is, not many companies are close to realizing it. They find it hard to change, in part just because old habits die hard and in part because every company has well-entrenched practices and interests that get in the way of change. Promotions are handed out due to politics as well as for performance. Incentive systems continue to reward individual rather than team achievement. The demands of the day—get the product out the door, launch the new marketing campaign, meet the quarterly-earnings goal—overshadow the longer-term need for re-creation of the organization itself.

Executives leading the charge for change find themselves faced with dilemmas and contradictions, and just figuring out where to start the change process can be something of a puzzle. "ABB is an organization with three internal contradictions," said Percy Barnevik, former chief executive of the big industrial conglomerate. "We want to be global and local, big and small, and radically decentralized with centralized reporting and control. If we resolve those contradictions, we create real organizational advantage."[1] This may be true—and Barnevik enjoyed a notable reputation as a visionary leader—but it isn't exactly a recipe that someone in another company can follow.

At the end of 2001, the world had changed a great deal both organizationally and within individual homes. Owing to the unprecedented attacks of September 11, 2001, and subsequent recession, many workers have spent a lot of time re thinking their priorities. Businesses have had to change the way they manage their people. The year went from prosperity, in many cases, to very abrupt endings. What now? Organization must, by necessity, change or die as the Darwinian theory of natural selection goes.

To get a handle on organizational change, the most fruitful approach may be to look at organizations that *have* adapted to new realities—in some cases by wholly transforming themselves, in others by a more gradual process of evolution. Then we can see what lessons these pioneers may teach.

ADAPTING IN TIMES OF CRISIS

Arguably, airlines felt the greatest economic impact resulting directly from the 9/11 terrorist attacks. Yet although such an industry is prone to change, the core of the company's operations tends to remain fairly static. Adapting to the impact of sudden events is hard enough for even the most dynamic organization, but for monoliths like the major airlines, it seems practically impossible. When asked by *Fortune* magazine about the possibility of changing American Airlines's culture, a veteran flight attendant of the airline, Elaine Barber, responded that it "is like trying to turn around a ten-mile-long freight train."[2]

Though airlines are used to responding to the unexpected, at certain points even their own standard operating procedures are not effective enough. Northwest Airlines became embroiled in a lawsuit, eventually settled for $7.1 million, after Northwest's slow response to a January 1999 snowstorm caused more than 7,000 passengers to be trapped aboard 30 airplanes for upwards of 2.5 hours and, in some cases, over 8 hours when planes could not take off and could not return to the gates. Toilets overflowed, planes ran out of food and water, and there were several reports of passengers being told to remain in their seats despite how long they were stranded. Because the airline was unable to make decisions quickly enough to free the passengers, Northwest's customers were forced to endure the problems caused by large organizations that are not able to respond quickly.

In the case of American Airlines on September 11, the teams that normally would assist NTSB investigators were not allowed to go to crash sites because they were considered crime scenes by authorities. The teams that would normally rush to aid victims' families couldn't get there soon enough, because all flights were banned. And, like all the airlines, crews were scattered across the country, as were their planes.

Still American Airlines scrambled to meet the needs of the crisis. Among other responses, within the week of the disaster, American had set up a hot line dedicated to answering the crews' questions, and still another phone bank, with the help of the APFA (Association of Professional Flight Attendants) to quickly add badly needed counseling resources. As airports reopened, new schedules, which normally take months to create, were created and changed again as various new information came to light.

Clearly these examples are the extremes of organizations' need to be adaptive. However, they still bring to mind the ever-changing environment we live in, and the preparations that must be undertaken by businesses in order to respond and survive.

VIVENDI UNIVERSAL:
THE POWERFUL TRANSFORMATION

First the company was called Compagnie Générale des Eaux (General Water Company). Established in 1853 by an imperial decree, it supplied water to Paris, Lyons, Venice, and Constantinople. After a century, the company's interests had spread to water treatment, district heating networks, household-waste incineration, and composting plants. In 1983 it branched out still farther, creating a joint venture called Canal +—the first encrypted pay-television channel in France—and, four years later, a mobile-telephone company. It became the European leader in waste management. It added interests in construction and civil engineering.

Then, in 1998, Jean-Marie Messier became chief executive officer. A onetime treasury official and investment banker, the man who would become one of France's first (and few) superstar CEOs moved to diversify still more. He changed the company's name to the more up-to-date (and less specific) Vivendi. He increased his stake in Canal

+ while selling off other business units. He teamed up with Vodafone, the mobile-phone leader in the United Kingdom, to create a Web portal called Vizzavi.[3] Meanwhile he put the utility-style businesses, such as water and waste management, into a separate division called Vivendi Environment and loaded up that division with most of the company's $17 billion in debt. That drove the stock price of his media-and-communications division up, and he used the appreciated stock to buy the Canadian giant Seagram, owner of Hollywood hit factory Universal Studios and market leader Universal Music. Nor did he stop there. In 2001 he bought Houghton Mifflin, a billion-dollar U.S. publisher with a sizable textbook business; MP3.com, which will provide the technology for an online music service; a Moroccan telephone company; and other businesses.

Messier's creation: Vivendi Universal, the world's second-largest media group, a global entertainment company rivaling Disney, Viacom, and AOL Time Warner.

At this writing, Vivendi's immediate prospects are uncertain. The company's stock lost a lot of its value during 2001, like the stock of other media businesses, and many analysts worried that Messier was piling up too much debt in pursuit of a strategy that seemingly lacked coherence. Still, Messier seemed to have a keen appreciation of the full range of his company's assets. Vivendi Environment—72 percent owned by Vivendi Universal—continued to generate large amounts of cash, and had long-term contracts with the likes of Hyundai Petrochemical, which was paying the company a billion euros over twenty years for waste-water treatment. It's a "big chunk of Vivendi Universal's revenue and earnings stream," reported the *Wall Street Journal*.[4] Vivendi Environment was scheduled to be listed on the New York Stock Exchange in fall 2001. Meanwhile, Universal Studios was cranking out a series of hits, and Universal Music held some 22 percent of global album sales. Analysts pointed out that Messier could raise more cash for acquisitions by downgrading its debt and refinancing its commercial paper with bank debt—though that would both increase its cost of capital and give the banks a bigger role in the company's future.[5]

A recipe for long-term success? No one can say. But Messier's bold moves put Vivendi onto a possible fast track—and left behind forever its slow-growth legacy as a 150-year-old water company.

Nokia

Nokia was originally the name of a wood-pulp mill in southern Finland that sold paper and cardboard. A town grew up around the mill, and that, too, was called Nokia. Around the turn of the twentieth century a company called Finnish Rubber Works—its main product was rubber boots—opened a plant in the town, eventually merging with the paper company. In the 1920s the Rubber Works began using Nokia as a brand name. In the late 1940s, after World War II, it bought majority ownership in another company, Finnish Cable Works, which made cables for telephone and telegraph networks. In 1967 the Nokia Group was formed out of all these disparate components. It was a stolid, sleepy conglomerate selling rubber goods, lumber and paper products, cable, and many other items, much of it going to the Soviet Union.

Today, of course, Nokia is the market leader in the cutting-edge technology sector of mobile telephony. As of this writing its market share is 35 percent, about three times the volume of Motorola, its nearest competitor.[6]

What a transformation! But like a lot of dramatic stories in life, this one didn't just happen. Nokia's change had its origin in the company's roots, in economic necessity, and in visionary leadership.

Roots

When the Nokia Group was formed in 1967, it included a small electronics division. The division introduced so-called pulse-code modulation telephone equipment and became a leader in radio telephony, a technology important to sparsely populated Scandinavia. It supplied telephones to Ericsson, Sweden's giant telephone-equipment maker, for an early cellular network in 1980. One technological advance followed another. The Talkman, introduced in 1984, weighed close to 5 kilos (11 lbs.), though it was advanced for its time. The Cityman, in 1987, weighed less than one kilo. In the late 1980s and early 1990s Nokia became a leader in GSM (Global System for Mobile Communications) technology, and in 1991 made an agreement to supply GSM networks to nine other European countries.

Economic Necessity (and Opportunity)

When the Soviet Union collapsed, one of Nokia's largest markets shrank drastically—leaving it, among other troubles, with a mass of unsellable toilet paper.[7] At the same time, the demand for mobile phones operating on the new GSM digital standard was beginning to skyrocket. The only problem was manufacturing: "Nokia had so little idea about how to raise production to meet demand that its mobile phone operation was nearly sold."[8]

Leadership

Jorma Ollila became chief executive of Nokia in 1992. Together with CFO Olli-Pekka Kallasvuo, he essentially gambled everything on a reinvention of the company. He sold off everything except cell phones and related infrastructure equipment. He invested heavily in new technologies, making the systems ever more sophisticated and the phones themselves ever smaller and more versatile. He built a culture—the "Nokia Way"—that is known for experimentation, continuous learning, and social responsibility. He branded the phones, emphasizing design and style, thereby turning them into fashion accessories as much as communications tools.

Nokia today remains a gamble. It is vulnerable to technological evolution as well as to attacks by powerful competitors from both the United States and Japan. Its stock reflects the volatility of the telecom sector in general. Internally, CEO Ollila says its biggest threat is "complacency."[9] But Nokia has a variety of strengths to draw on in addition to its technological leadership and culture. Its network infrastructure business grew by 35 percent in the first quarter of 2001. Nokia dipped its toes into the difficult but increasingly essential task of financing sales to cell-phone network vendors, thereby picking up a couple of percentage points of market share. On the cell phone front itself, Nokia maintains its position as low-cost manufacturer and expects its market share to increase to 40 percent. It has created a portal called Club Nokia to provides services to owners of its phones.[10]

In short, Nokia's transformation continues, albeit on a far narrower basis. Meanwhile, it has been named by Interbrand—the global brand-valuation firm—as the fifth most valuable brand in the world, following only Coca-Cola, Microsoft, IBM, and Intel.[11] Quite a change from a paper mill or a rubber-boot company.

BUILDING THE ADAPTABLE COMPANY

Adaptive companies such as these are the organizations that will survive in the future. Building one—turning a conventional company into one that is truly adaptive—entails understanding these organizations' three key characteristics.

Learning

The term "learning organization" was coined some years ago by management theorist Peter Senge. Human beings are born learners, says Senge, but the social and organizational structures in which we're raised and socialized tend to shift our natural learning abilities into something narrower and less rewarding. We learn to adapt, to get along, rather than to exercise our creative powers. We learn to seek the approval of others. By channeling our desire to learn into such unproductive paths, companies create the precise environment and conditions that produce mediocre or poor performance.

Today, says Senge, the universe we must work in is increasingly dynamic, interdependent, and unpredictable. It's no longer possible for any one individual or small group to "figure it all out"; instead, we need to integrate thinking and acting at all levels of the organization. New opportunities must be explored even while old ways are maintained. Creative learning as well as adaptive learning must be encouraged. Leaders must take responsibility not only for their own learning but for helping people to expand their own horizons and the horizons of their company.[12]

A Connected Organization

As businesses work toward adaptability, they must make a variety of changes. One key point: building strong working relationships, both inside and outside the organization. Relationships provide feedback, along with criticism of, or resistance to, a proposed course of action. Companies that want to learn must welcome such resistance and opposition rather than attempt to quell it. An organization must also respect—and keep informed—everyone who has stake in the outcome of the business, such as employees, customers, investors, and prospective investors. The challenges in all this? One is to maintain focus. "While focusing near and far at the same time is difficult," said change specialist Rick Maurer, "plans should include ways to keep your sights clearly on both the goal and the current situation." In addition, company leadership needs to stay "relaxed." Writes Maurer: "If change leaders feel off-balance, they could lash out and ruin any chance for collaboration."[13]

A Flexible and Informed Organization

An adaptive organization possesses certain key characteristics, wrote William E. Fulmer in his book *Shaping the Adaptive Organization*.[14] An adaptive organization is decentralized. Multiple groups and individuals are involved in decision-making. Such companies allow people broader spans of control. (Fulmer: "Increasing the span of control reduces hierarchy, gives more people a role in decision making and helps identify and develop good executives.") Adaptive organizations make as much use as possible of temporary structures, outsourcing noncore elements of the business, forming alliances, and using teams. The trait that emerges from all these characteristics is flexibility. It's precisely because an adaptive company isn't centrally controlled—because it relies on a broad range of people to make decisions, and because these employees don't try to do everything themselves—that it can move much faster than a traditional organization. Of course, it doesn't work unless the company incorporates powerful information systems that keep everyone informed. Technology allows people to exchange information, learn from one another, and thereby make better decisions.

Put these traits together and you come up with an organization that looks and feels like a Nokia or a Vivendi—a company that has remained true to its values and focused in its determination to satisfy the demands of its shareholders, employees, and other stakeholders even if that means morphing from old businesses (like water or rubber boots) to new businesses (like telecom) as drivers of economic value change. Such companies are well suited to make the transition from competition in the twentieth century to competition in the twenty-first century.

Adaptation never ends. Whether in times of crisis or just the normal speed of change, businesses, like any other species, must constantly evolve and grow or they will not survive.

PART THREE

Putting It All Together

MANAGING YOUR
COMPANY'S INTANGIBLES

In part one of this book we defined intangibles and offered a brief history of the role they have played in business. We explained both why that role is changing and why it's growing more important every day. One conclusion of our research was that large institutional investors already utilize intangibles in making investment choices—in fact, intangibles account for as much as 35 percent of these decisions. Another was that intangibles often make the difference between a successful and an unsuccessful IPO.

In part two we provided a list of twelve intangibles we believe are the primary drivers of value creation in corporations. We deliberately painted these with a broad brush and assembled a wide range of evidence as to their importance. Some readers will want to change the list a little; others will insist on different titles or descriptions. No matter. As we said elsewhere, we do not pretend to be the final word on this subject or to have the perfect answer. Nor do we think you should trust anyone who says he or she does. The field is too new, and everyone in it is continuing to learn from each other.

The real issue, at any rate, isn't whether you use one term or another but how you manage intangibles so as to optimize their value, and thus the value of your company. The challenge for any business today is not just to understand intangibles but to *utilize* them to attain—and maintain—what we have been calling an invisible advantage. This part of the book will outline a series of practical steps to help you get started.

MAKING THE CASE FOR MANAGING INTANGIBLES

Most companies don't easily embark on *any* new approach to management. There's the press of daily business. There's a reluctance among many people even to consider doing things differently. Intangibles in particular may be greeted with skepticism. "Hard-nosed" businesspeople have learned to manage financial results, period. Someone who suggests they should start to pay attention to "soft" measures such as employee satisfaction or the company's ability to adapt may not get the positive reaction he or she hopes for. We can almost hear it now: One More Fad. Flavor of the Month.

But it's a big mistake to regard intangibles as just another fad, and not only because outside investors are already utilizing them in making their decisions. Let us tell you a couple of stories that show just how important intangibles can be. Maybe they'll help you persuade your colleagues.

In 1998—with encouragement from the magazine *Forbes ASAP* and technical assistance from professors at the University of Pennsylvania's Wharton School—we put a quick-and-dirty survey up on the Web. Explaining that the survey was really to guide the more formal research that would follow, we asked any businesspeople who were interested to participate. The questions were simple. We just asked respondents to tell us what the key *drivers of value* were in their companies—the financial and nonfinancial factors that they thought really helped them create value as managers. Then we asked what sorts of information they were getting that helped them measure and understand those value drivers, and whether they were satisfied with the quality of the information. The results surprised us: Some 81 percent of respondents told us that they got very poor information on the value drivers—on the very things that they thought were most important to them as managers.

A couple of months later we were invited to speak at a *Forbes* executive conference in Naples, Florida. The audience was made up entirely of CEOs and high-level executives. The conference organizers suggested we use the automatic audience response system that was part of the conference to try our survey out with them. Frankly, we were dubious. The people in that audience, we reasoned, were the people who *create* the systems of information and measurement in their companies. Surely they would be satisfied with information that was being provided. We figured we'd just spend an hour debating with them, and then go home. We were surprised again: Fully 71 percent of the people in this audience of chief and senior executives told us that the information they were providing and receiving was extremely poor. They felt that they weren't giving or getting the kind of information that they and their subordinates needed to manage their companies.

These results suggested to us that a lot of managers in large corporations were suffering from a sizable information gap. To figure out just how bad it was, we launched a study that came to be known as *Decisions That Matter*. We wanted to identify the critical nonfinancial drivers of long-term economic value from the perspective of senior managers. We also wanted to assess the performance consequences of gaps between value drivers and the use of measures for internal decision-making and external reporting. In other words, were executives in different industries getting good information about the factors they identified as important, or was there a gap? And if there was, did it really matter? That is, was the gap reflected in a company's financial performance?

What we found was unambiguous. A majority of executives in *every* industry we studied believed that there were disconnects— gaps—between the drivers they felt were critical to the company's success and what was actually being measured and reported. What's more, *smaller gaps went hand in hand with better financial performance* as measured by return on assets, five-year net-income growth, and higher stock returns (in both one-year and three-year increments). It's difficult to get much harder-nosed than that.

Are these results surprising? Certainly tradition-minded executives might be astonished to learn, for example, that better assessment of a financial services company's environmental practices correlates with hard measures of its financial performance. But think for a moment about all the changes in the business landscape over the past couple of decades. Major investors such as Salomon Smith Barney and the California Public Employees Retirement System (CalPERS) now consider just such variables in making their investment decisions. Companies perform due diligence on areas such as employee relations in scrutinizing business partners. For example, Citizens Bank of Canada's ethics policy states that it "will not invest in or do business with any company that has a poor record of employee relations in the areas of health and safety, labour practices, employee benefits, or employment equity."[1]

Our next study made the case for intangibles even stronger. In effect, we learned that it's possible to create an index assessing companies' performance on a wide variety of intangibles. We also learned that companies' "score" on this index—their score on intangibles management, so to speak—has a direct, measurable effect on their market valuations.

First, we identified nine critical nonfinancial drivers based on previous research. Then we chose various universes of companies to study. Originally we focused on S&P 500 manufacturing companies—companies with at least $100 million in market capitalization. Later we studied individual industries such as financial services and telecommunications.

Next, we gathered data about each of the drivers. The data came from both public and proprietary sources, and included information from government filings, special studies, company reports, and ratings by industry experts. Where possible, we used multiple indicators from different sources to evaluate each category; doing so provided a more comprehensive and reliable assessment of a company's overall performance on any given dimension. For example, the driver *al-*

liances comprised five indicators: number of alliances, number of alliance partners, number of supplier partners, number of marketing agreements, and number of joint ventures.

Finally, we ran the numbers. Through rigorous (and tedious!) quantitative analysis, we confirmed that the multiple indicators we were using to measure each driver were statistically related and in fact captured the same underlying value driver category. We also weighted the drivers into an overall score, which we called a *value creation index*, or VCI. The "VCI scores" we computed were essentially a measure of companies' performance on these intangible dimensions.

The results of this study were even more powerful than those of the first. The VCI demonstrated that *at least 50 percent of a traditional company's value is based on these nine drivers*. For both durable and nondurable manufacturers, VCI score was highly correlated—0.70—with market value. In fact, a company's VCI score correlated as strongly with its market value as did its financial performance. What's more, improvement in key intangible drivers translated strongly into increased market value. Relatively small changes in the VCI can produce significant changes in market value; a 10-percent change in VCI score—either up or down—is associated with a 5-percent change in market value—correspondingly up or down, after controlling for financial variables. In our study of manufacturers, this corresponded to a $3.9-billion increase in market value in the durable-goods sector and a $2.2-billion increase for the nondurable-goods sector.

The VCI also shows the relative importance of the intangibles used to create it. For both groups of manufacturers, for instance, innovation was the most important single intangible. Innovation was defined in this case by factors such as the number of U.S. patents held by a company, its R&D expenditures, and certain innovation and patent-importance rankings. Quality of management and employee relations were also among the top three intangibles in both groups. Maybe that confirms the truth of the corporate cliché "people are our most important asset."

When we compiled VCIs for companies in individual industries, we were able to drill down even deeper into exactly which intangibles make the most difference. In a study of e-commerce companies, for instance—remember them?—we used seven drivers, including four that were unique to this business. Here, alliances, innovation, and "eyes" on the Web site proved to be the highest-ranking drivers. In an eerily prescient view of what would unfold a year later, we found that brand and "stickiness," the amount of time a person spent at a given Web site, were not particularly strong indicators of value. In a study of telecommunications companies, we found that five intangibles—employee talent, management quality, brand strength, workplace environment, and technological innovation—are all significant drivers of market value. (They're listed in order of importance.) In fact, about 85 percent of a given company's market value can be explained by the intangible drivers of this industry.

The telecom study—completed in October 2000—also turned up fascinating insights about individual companies. For instance, we noticed that the market caps of Motorola, Lucent, AT&T, NTT, Nortel, and Cisco seemed well above what was warranted by their VCI scores. Sure enough: By February 2001 all six companies saw their market values plunge by at least 22 percent. (By contrast, several companies whose market caps were *below* what was warranted by their VCI, including Telecom Italia and Bellsouth, saw positive growth.) The most dramatic decline? Lucent, whose VCI score ranked it twenty-first out of the twenty-two companies we studied, lost close to 50 percent of its value by February 2001. Anecdotal evidence suggests why. Employee talent is the most important VCI category in this industry, and Lucent has been doing "a poor job of incorporating talent into the company."[2] ("Who wants to work at Lucent?" said a Cascade Communications veteran who left after his company was bought by Lucent.) A second problem: a low score on management quality, which ranks as the second most important value driver. Since October 2000, Lucent experienced a major shake-up in its management, culminating in the ousting of its CEO, and was targeted by the Securities and Exchange Commission for an investigation into possible fraudulent accounting practices.

MANAGING INTANGIBLES: THE FIVE KEY STEPS

Once people understand evidence such as this, the job of persuading them of the importance of intangibles becomes significantly easier. This is all to the good, because what we think most businesses need is a *companywide commitment to managing intangibles*—to identifying them, assessing them, and learning to improve them. That's the true source of invisible advantage: measuring and rewarding improvements in the real drivers of a company's value.

Every organization is different, and we don't mean to oversimplify what can be a difficult process of learning to manage your intangibles. But our research has identified five broad steps that no company can avoid.

1. Determine the Critical Intangibles for Your Business

Virtually every industry has three or four intangibles that wind up being the most important. We studied half a dozen different industries, and we rarely found consistency in the rankings. In manufacturing, as noted above, innovation, quality of management, and employee relations were most important, while technology and customer satisfaction ranked low. In financial services, the top rankers were management quality, technology, brand, and customer relations. (Alliances were important in financial services, too—but a high score on the alliance scale was *negatively* correlated with market cap.) In airlines, employee quality was far and away the single most important driver of value.

How to determine your own key intangibles? We suspect that most seasoned executives already have a sense of what's important to them. Just as savvy managers often keep a private desk-drawer tally of key operational or financial ratios, they often have a gut feel for the intangibles that matter. A plant manager might watch absenteeism or defect rates as a gauge of employee morale. An R&D manager might keep an eye on the number of new projects starting up each quarter. A marketing vice president might tally customer complaints or Web-site visits.

Of course, the most important intangible for an individual manager or department may not be the most important for a company, or even for a business unit. So here's what we recommend: ask the leadership team to come up with rankings of the intangibles they believe are most important for the business as a whole. Get the group together and put them up on a whiteboard. Challenge—and ask people to defend—every one. Don't stop until you've arrived at a rough consensus. The key question is this: What are the real drivers of value in *our* business? If we could gain a competitive advantage by improving our performance in two or three key areas, what would they be?

Tip: Don't rely on input only from three or four senior leaders. Get as many experienced managers as you can into the discussion. The consensus will be that much broader, and the decisions that much better.

2. Decide on Metrics for the Key Intangibles

When it comes to metrics, the first question for most companies is what they already measure. Often somebody somewhere in the organization is gathering valuable data that gets filed away, and that can be utilized. For example, many companies gather up all kinds of statistics about their customers' satisfactions and dissatisfactions, but never compile it into an index that shows how effectively they are managing their brands.

So gather up that data—and if there's information you need that you don't have, figure out how to get it. Some intangibles lend themselves to relatively easy measurement. Like customers, for instance, employees can be polled about how satisfied they are. Human-resources indicators like turnover can be easily tracked. Similarly, analysts and journalists can be polled as to the quality of a company's communication. Other intangibles present more of a challenge. "Leadership quality" is often tough to gauge (and ticklish to discuss!). "Workplace organization and culture" is a broad intangible that encompasses several different sorts of metrics.

But "tough" doesn't mean "impossible." Take leadership, for instance. Are your company's leaders well respected in the industry? Can you point to specific recruitment and management-training programs that are held up as exemplars? Are departing leaders routinely sought for high-level jobs elsewhere? Are leaders routinely expected to train one or two possible successors? On the workplace-organization front, does your company make any "best place to work" lists? If there's a union, are labor relations generally smooth and negotiations productive? Do you rate high on employee involvement and participation? The answers to such questions often involve judgment, but that's no reason not to make them. Where appropriate, poll your customers, suppliers, investors, employees, and other stakeholders.

Tip: In measurement, the perfect is the enemy of the good. Identify a few metrics even if you think they leave something to be desired, then work on improving or replacing them over time.

3. Create a Baseline—and Benchmark It Against Your Competition

Ultimately, you want a "movie" of your management of intangibles; you want to see whether and how they are improving. But the first step is simply to take a snapshot of where you stand today, then assess your standing relative to competitors. The purpose of managing intangibles, after all, isn't simply to get better scores, it's to outflank your competitors with moves that are difficult or impossible to copy. So you need to know where your competitors' strengths and weaknesses are, and to gauge them against your own.

This can involve a substantial amount of research—and at the risk of tooting our profession's horn, this is where an outside consultant can often be helpful. Experienced consultants know what measures to look for. They're familiar with available industry data. They can conduct surveys of third parties, asking them to assess your performance on a variety of scales against the performance of your competitors. Good consultants are also more objective than most people inside a company can be.

Tip: Whether from a consultant or your own people, insist on brutal honesty. Intangibles are too important to fudge, or to play politics with. Remember Enron, Xerox, and other companies that tried to bury the truth: It doesn't work. The markets are too well informed and too relentless to be fooled for long.

4. Undertake Initiatives to Improve Your Performance on Key Intangibles

In the end, this is what it's all about. Intangibles can be *managed*. Your performance can be improved. Assessing and measuring your intangibles helps you determine where to invest time and resources. Undertaking initiatives to improve performance helps you build value.

Consider innovation, which ranks as one of the most important intangibles in many industries. Innovation entails R&D, to be sure. One measure of your success at R&D is the number of patents your company holds; a second is the number of new products in the pipeline; a third is the proportion of revenues and profits accounted for by products or services that are less than (say) three years old. Tracking several such measures—and setting yearly targets for improvement—will focus people's attention on them. But a focus on innovation extends well beyond R&D, and can affect how every department does its work. Are there new customer segments that you can serve simply by creating a new marketing campaign? Are there process improvements that can reduce costs or speed up throughput? Can the finance department develop new ways to better its cash-management performance? Intangibles such as innovation permeate a company, and focusing on them should affect how every business unit and department are managed. So every business unit and department should be expected to come up with initiatives.

Tip: Tie improvement on intangible drivers to managers' compensation. Period.

5. Communicate What You're Doing—Far and Wide

One of the themes of this book is has been that the returns to transparency exceed the returns to secrecy. If we ever needed an object lesson to this effect, the fall of Enron provided one. The company was regularly lauded in business books for its innovative culture and adaptability. For a while it was extraordinarily successful. But the company's success turned out to be built on something like a house of cards, and investors didn't know it because so many of Enron's dealings were cloaked in secrecy. They were mentioned, if at all, in footnotes to the financials. The language and paper trail were so obscure that even sophisticated Wall Street analysts didn't know what was going on. (Indeed, there is some question as to whether senior management really understood all of the company's operations.) When the market discovered the truth, the reaction was swift and severe.

The antithesis to such secrecy—and a kind of watchword for any company that wants to manage its intangibles effectively—is *open systems*. Share your insights into intangibles with employees, customers, suppliers, industry groups, investors, and Wall Street analysts. Share your metrics and your targets; let them know what you expect to achieve and why it's important. Don't worry about spilling your secrets—the information itself has limited competitive value. It's what you do with the information that matters. If you can show why a particular intangible is important, and if you can then improve your company's performance, you will gain credibility—and you will be rewarded for it by the market.

Tip: Consider adding an "intangibles audit" to your annual report. The audit can spell out your thinking about intangibles, communicate your goals, and assess your performance.

❀   ❀   ❀

We mentioned above that the study of intangibles is a new field, and it's a point that bears repeating. The fundamental ideas of this field are still gelling. The data are frequently spotty and difficult to compare across companies or industries. We think the research efforts and analyses we have outlined in this book are sound, but we urge you to experiment and test other models as well. Most executives already realize how inadequate the current system of measurement and disclosure is—just look at all the metaphors and analogies that are used to describe it ("steering by the ship's wake," "driving by looking at the rearview mirror," and so on). The technological innovations and rapid globalization of the last decade of the twentieth century have only exacerbated the information asymmetries that affect access to and costs of capital. When Warren Buffett, one of the wealthiest men in the United States and surely its most well-known investor, said, "If markets were efficient, I'd still have to work for a living," he was referring to precisely the dearth of good information about what really drives business decisions. The use of intangibles, once widely adopted, can provide better information.

But the relative novelty of intangibles shouldn't blind you to the need for action now. This isn't an area in which you can afford to sit back and wait for others to take the lead and for standards to emerge. The management of intangibles provides an important kind of first-mover advantage: Those who take the lead will *set* the standards. They will be appreciated as innovators and rewarded accordingly. They will be ahead of the pack, and the followers may find themselves hard-pressed to catch up. So it's important to make a start. As we have said repeatedly, the markets are making decisions about your intangibles every day—yet very few managers are engaged in defining, measuring, and disclosing what *they* consider important or worthy of analysis. There is probably no other field of managerial endeavor in which executives cede so much authority to those outside their organization. Why should they do so here?

We recognize that there are no easy or final answers. But we believe that whatever you do in this realm will be an improvement over the incomplete and frequently misleading picture painted by traditional financial measures. The legendary economist John Maynard Keynes once said, "I would rather be vaguely right than precisely wrong." We agree.

AFTERWORD

Any author takes a risk in writing a book such as this. The risk is that the process of marshaling arguments, gathering data, and then writing it all down becomes so all-consuming that you lose touch with the forces and trends that originally inspired the effort. As we began the book, we were mindful of all the discounted remainder bins in bookstores filled with volumes titled "e-this" or "Net-that"—books commissioned at the height of the dot-com bubble, twelve to eighteen months before the whole thing collapsed, and now no more relevant than yesterday's newspaper.

But as we complete this venture in the autumn of 2001, a number of developments—announced after we began writing—lead us to believe that the forces we are writing about are as strong as ever. Indeed, the importance of intangibles in the life of businesses and the people who work for them seems only to have grown. For instance:

- The European Commission issued a request for proposals for a study on "the measurement of intangible assets and associated accounting practices." Among the reasons cited, the EC noted that the growth differential between industrialized countries in the 1990s was explainable only if intangibles were taken into account. Said Mario Monti, competition commissioner for the European Union: "Protection of intellectual property [is] necessary to encourage creativity and investment . . . both of which are crucial for job creation and long term competitiveness."

- The government of Brazil stripped pharmaceutical giant Roche of its patent on the anti-AIDS drug Nelfinavir in a dispute over the price Roche was charging for access to the medication. Brazil's health minister justified the action by referring to a clause in Brazil's intellectual-property law that permits patents to be broken in cases of national emergency or abusive pricing. Although Brazil and Roche eventually negotiated a resolution, Roche was forced to make concessions. In November 2001, poor countries won the right to ignore drug company patents for a wide range of diseases. Negotiating at the World Trade Organization meeting in Qatar, the poor countries struck a deal that gives them the right to make or purchase generic drugs to address "health emergencies" through the grant of compulsory licenses. Each country has the right to define health emergency as it sees fit, underscoring the fragility of intellectual-property protections.
- The U.S. Federal Reserve, in its annual summer conference at Jackson Hole, Wyoming, chose in 2001 to grapple with "how intellectual property businesses are changing the fundamental dynamics of the market economy." This event, hosted by the Federal Reserve Bank of Kansas City, has in the past been noted for its consideration of such policy priorities as the nation's health insurance crisis. That the role of intangibles was the subject under discussion at this august forum suggests how topical it has become.
- UNESCO, the United Nations Educational, Scientific and Cultural Organization, announced a new addition to its World Heritage List. Known as the institution that has bestowed official recognition on sites such as Machu Picchu in Peru and the pyramids in Egypt, UNESCO designates places of "exceptional universal value" for inclusion on the list. The agency's director general, Koichiro Matsuura, became concerned that such designations should not be

awarded solely to cultural or natural nominees of a tangible nature. Consequently, UNESCO is set to announce its list of Masterpieces of the Oral and Intangible Heritage of Humanity. It is worth noting that this gentle global organization dedicated to the advancement of knowledge and culture shares an interest with the world of business in recognizing, among other intangibles, "the values and know-how of human communities."

Unfortunately, the most momentous and horrifying evidence of intangibles' impact occurred on September 11, 2001, when the infamous suicide attack destroyed the World Trade Center in New York City and damaged part of the Pentagon just outside Washington, D.C. In some ways the attack was (at this writing) only the latest and most devastating reflection of the rising tide of resentment in the world against U.S. economic leadership and what is loosely referred to as globalization. Vast and often violent demonstrations in Seattle, Washington, Goteborg, and Genoa had signaled popular discomfort with the trends of commercialization. Still, no amount of resentment or frustration could account for the horror brought on by the attacks.

What the attacks do indicate, however, is indisputable: the triumph of belief systems over information systems. The terrorists understood very well the power of symbolism. They struck with extraordinary precision at the preeminent physical manifestations of American business and military power. In a stroke they rejected the values and norms of the West—the sanctity of human life, the inviolability of innocents in war, and many other painstakingly codified standards by which this civilization has thought to differentiate itself from a savage but supposedly distant past. In so doing the terrorists compounded the shock and disarray of their designated enemies. The vulnerability of our system to this sort of once-unthinkable assault was both a weapon they employed and a lesson they successfully imparted.

In visiting so damaging a physical and psychological blow on the culture and economy they despised, this small band of fanatics relied on little that was tangible. They were apparently poorly capitalized. They ignored advanced technologies—missiles, for example—that might have been available to them. They marshaled not vast armies but a small, committed cadre. They used not weapons of mass destruction—not even firearms—but the lineal descendent of one of mankind's oldest tools, the knife.

In place of tangible weaponry or forces, they wielded a dazzling array of intangibles: leadership, organization, alliances and networks, human capital, and culture. They were even more or less transparent in the way they prepared, understanding that the culture they were attacking prized the very openness they used against it. And even the economic cost of the attack must be measured most heavily in intangibles: people lost, relationships severed. Said Cliff Rackson, a financial trader, "There's capital and there's human talent. That's all Wall Street is. So how do you replace all that lost human talent?"[1]

Much has and will be written about the causes, effects, and potential implications of this event. Our purpose in writing about it is not to offer a treatise on military history or counterterrorism. We mention it only because because the people who committed these crimes against humanity understood the power of intangibles in our society better than many of us do ourselves. They used that knowledge against us to devastating effect.

Our belief is that businesses must learn from this as they must from any well-known success or infamous disaster. Along with the horror and devastation the event brought, it also brought a reminder of how intangibles are playing a greater role—for good or ill—in all of our lives. The implicit warning is that we not become the sort of person described by Oscar Wilde, the English writer: "A cynic is a man who knows the price of everything and the value of nothing."

❀   ❀   ❀

To return once more to the everyday world: Our goal in writing this book has been to explain the growing importance of intangibles and to help managers do something about it. We have tried to demonstrate that the existing systems for measuring and disclosing corporate performance no longer adequately reflect the underlying economic activity they were designed to represent. Through our own research and that of colleagues, as well as through our experience in working with clients, we have sought to explain *how* intangibles have assumed this growing role, *why* some intangibles have become particularly important to corporations, and *what* managers can do about it.

The twelve intangibles we have highlighted appear to us to be the most important right now. We believe that over time, with further research and practical experience, some of the factors on our list will be replaced by others. In fact, we would be disappointed if that did not happen. We say this because we believe that the constantly evolving and adaptive nature of our economy and the organizations that contribute to it will demand that kind of iterative process. Increased knowledge creates a push for more of the same. We do not believe it is either advisable or possible to create a successor to the 500-year-old accounting system based on the discovery of double-entry bookkeeping by medieval monks.

But we do believe in the power of ideas, of the people who generate them, and of the networks that connect them to provide positive change and the possibility of growth. A possibly apocryphal story about Pablo Picasso, arguably the greatest artist of the twentieth century, illustrates this point. A tourist approached Picasso at a café in Paris and asked him to draw her likeness, offering to pay him a fair price when he was done. Picasso agreed and finished the sketch in a matter of minutes. When she asked what she owed him, he told her 5,000 francs.

She expressed surprise at the price. "But it only took you a few minutes," she said.

"No," Picasso replied. "It took me all my life."

The implications for business? There is considerable unseen and unrecognized value—an invisible advantage—in the ideas and people who make up the organizations through which we manage our world. Whether they be public, private, or not-for-profit, these organizations can benefit from the identification, measurement, and management of the kinds of intangibles we have highlighted in this book. The responsibility for taking steps toward this goal rests first and foremost with those who are charged with the management of these enterprises. A growing acknowledgment of the beneficial power of good corporate governance has stimulated this movement, and will continue to do so. However, people elsewhere in an organization—whether it's a tightly run corporation or a loosely knit network—don't need to wait for senior executives. They can begin right now to contribute to the understanding and management of the intangibles that, increasingly, will determine their organizations' future.

NOTES

CHAPTER 1

1. Daniel Gross and the editors of *Forbes* magazine, *Forbes' Greatest Business Stories of All Time*, New York, John Wiley & Sons, 1996, p. 184–186.
2. *Pfizer 2000 Annual Report*, p. 2.
3. Lynn J. Lundsford, "Pratt & Whitney Tries to Prove Its Glory Days Aren't Past," *Wall Street Journal*, August 14, 2001.
4. GE Healthcare Financial Services: Financing Case Studies(http://www.gemedicalsystems.com/services/financial/case_studies/surg_amb.html).
5. Karl Taro Greenfeld, "Battle Deluxe Titans LVMH and Gucci Vie for Dominance in the Fashion World," *Time*, April 23, 2000.
6. Anonymous, "Face Value: The Cashmere Revolutionary," *The Economist*, July 15, 2000, p. 66.
7. Greenfeld, "Battle Deluxe Titans LVMH and Gucci Vie for Dominance in the Fashion World."
8. "What Risks Do Companies Face in Today's Economy," *Fortune*, February 7, 2000.
9. Abstracted from *La Tribune* in French, *World Reporter,* "Christian Sautter Deprives Coca-Cola of Orangina," *La Tribune,* November 25, 1999.
10. Carol Hymowitz, "Some CEOs Fail to See Exit Sign," *Wall Street Journal,* April 24, 2000.
11. Jay Weiner, "Good for A-Rod, Bad for Baseball," *Business Week,* December 25, 2000, p. 59.
12. Paul Keegan, "The Office That Ozzie Built," *New York Times*, October 23, 1995.

13. Howard R. Gold, "A Return Visit to Earlier Stories—The Lotus Eater: Manzi Leaves IBM, Wiser and a Lot Richer," *Barron's*, October 16, 1995.

14. Other firms took similar measures. See, for example, Douglas M. McCracken, "Winning the Talent War for Women," *Harvard Business Review* 78, no. 6 (November/December 2000): 159–67.

15. Again, CGEY wasn't alone. See Aaron Bernstein, "The Human Factor," *BusinessWeek*, August 27, 2001.

16. Aaron Bernstein, "The Human Factor," *BusinessWeek*, August 27, 2001.

17. Gary McWilliams, "Lean Machine: How Dell Fine-Tunes Its PC Pricing to Gain Edge in a Slow Market," *Wall Street Journal*, June 8, 2001, p. 1.

18. Shari Mycek, "Rolling Out the Red Carpet for Employees," *Trustee*, February 2000.

19. Assif Shameen, "After the Crash," Asia Week.com, vol. 26, no. 45, November 17, 2000.

Chapter 2

1. David A. Hounsell, *American System to Mass Production, 1800–1932*, Johns Hopkins University Press, 1984.

2. Henry Ford Museum & Greenfield Village, *The Life of Henry Ford* (http://www.hrmgv.org/histories/hf/chrono.html).

3. *A Science Odyssey: People and Discoveries: Henry Ford*.

4. Info on assembly line and productivity from James P. Womack, Daniel T. Jones, and Daniel Roos, *The Machine That Changed the World*, Rawson Associates, 1990, pp. 28ff. Price figures from the Lemelson-MIT Prize Program: Henry Ford.

5. David Montgomery, *The Fall of the House of Labor*, Cambridge University Press, 1987, p. 234.

6. Daniel Cross and the editors of *Forbes* Magazine, Forbes' *Greatest Business Stories of All Time*, John Wiley & Sons, 1996.

7. Alfred P. Sloan Foundation (http://www.sloan.org/sloanbio.shtml).

8. James P. Womack, Daniel T. Jones, and Daniel Roos, *The Machine That Changed the World*, HarperPerennial, 1991, p. 43.

9. Bureau of Labor Statistics Web site.

10. Thomas A. Stewart, "Accounting Gets Radical: The Green-Eyeshade Gang Isn't Measuring What Really Matters to Investors. Some Far-Out Thinkers Plan to Change That," *Fortune,* April 16, 2001.

11. World Trade Organization import and export data.

12. Ibid.

13. *Japan Auto Trends*, vol. 5, no. 1, March 2001. Japan Automobile Manufacturers Newsletter, "JAMA Members Set New Records in their purchase of US-Made Auto Parts."

14. John Case, "Who Wants to Be An Entrepreneur?" *Inc.*, May 15, 2001.

15. John Case, "Small Business 2001: Where We Are Now," *Inc.*, May 15, 2001.

16. "Sixth Annual State of Small Business Issue," *Inc.*, 2001, p. 77.

CHAPTER 3

1. Speech to the National Association for Business Economics, reported in "Greenspan Calls for Better Data Collection," *New York Times,* March 28, 2001.

2. "What Is the U.S. Gross Investment in Intangibles? (At Least One Trillion Dollars a Year)," Paper presented at the 4th Intangibles Conference on Advances in the Measurement of Intangible (Intellectual) Capital," New York University, May 17 and 18, 2001, and subsequent discussion.

3. Presentation to the 4th Intangibles Conference on Advances in the Measurement of Intangible (Intellectual) Capital, New York University, May 17 and 18, 2001, and subsequent discussion.

4. Speech to the National Association for Business Economics, reported in "Greenspan Calls for Better Data Collection," *New York Times,* March 28, 2001.

5. Thomas A. Stewart, "Accounting Gets Radical; The Green-Eyeshade Gang Isn't Measuring What Really Matters to Investors. Some Far-Out Thinkers Plan to Change That," *Fortune,* April 16, 2001.

6. Floyd Norris, "Seeking Ways to Value Intangible Assets," *New York Times*, May 22, 2001.

7. Wayne S. Upton, Jr., "Business and Financial Reporting, Challenges from the New Economy," Financial Accounting Standards Board, April 2001.

8. The Institute of Chartered Accountants in England & Wales, *Corporate Governance: The 21st Century Annual Report*, November 1998, p 2.

9. Clark Eustace, "The Intangible Economy—Impact and Policy Issues," *Report of the European High-Level Expert Group on the Intangible Economy,* European Commission, October 2000.

10. *Goodwill* represents the difference between the book value of an acquired company and what the buyer actually paid for it. That can produce absurd situations: In one case reported by the *Wall Street Journal,* an Internet consulting firm named MarchFirst bought another, named USWeb/CKS, and at the time the article was written still had $6.1 billion of goodwill from the acquisition on its books. Meanwhile, with Internet stocks out of favor, MarchFirst's market value had fallen to a measly $233 million—or about 1/26th of the value of the goodwill alone! Nor was this a problem confined to a small number of onetime high flyers. Aetna, the insurance company, was carrying $8.1 billion of goodwill on its balance sheet when its market cap was only $5.8 billion. For R. J. Reynolds Tobacco Company the corresponding figures were $7.4 billion and $5.0 billion.

11. Pallavi Gogoi, "Amazon.com's Junk Bonds Raise an Issue," *Wall Street Journal,* May 4, 1998.

12. "Improving Business Reporting—A Customer Focus," AICPA Special Committee on Financial Reporting (a.k.a. Jenkins Committee). The American Institute of Certified Public Accountants, 1991.

13. AIMR/FAPC92, p. 61. Finacial Accounting Policy Committee of the Association for Investment Management Research.

CHAPTER 4

1. See Anthony J. Rucci, Steven P. Kirn, Richard T. Quinn, "The Employee-Customer-Profit Chain at Sears," *Harvard Business Review,* January–February, 1998, p. 82–97.

2. Claes Fornell, "The Science of Satisfaction," *Harvard Business Review,* March 2001, p. 118.

3. Michael Arndt, "How O'Neill Got Alcoa Shining," *BusinessWeek,* February 5, 2001, p. 39.

4. Nicholas Stein, "The World's Most Admired Companies," *Fortune,* October 2, 2000, p. 182.

5. The Brookings Institution, "Understanding Intangible Sources of Value: Strategic and Organizational Issues Sub-group Report," 2000, p. 11.

6. National Science Foundation, "National Patterns of R&D Resources: 2000 Data Update," Table 1A.

7. The Brookings Institution, "Understanding Intangible Sources of Value: Strategic and Organizational Issues Sub-group Report," 2000, pp. 27–28.

8. "Nike Trips Over Its Laces," *BusinessWeek*, March 12, 2001.

CHAPTER 5

1. Geoffrey Colvin, "The Great CEO Pay Heist," *Fortune*, June 25, 2001, p. 64.

2. Ram Charan and Geoffrey Colvin, "The Right Fit," *Fortune,* April 17, 2000, p. 226

3. John Kenneth Galbraith, *The New Industrial State,* New York, Houghton Mifflin, 1967, p. 2.

4. John Kenneth Galbraith, *Economics and the Public Purpose*, New American Library, Part of Penguin Putnam, Inc., NY: 1973, p. 92.

5. "Face Value: The Wrong Trousers," *The Economist*, June 16, 2001, p. 68.

6. See, for example, Daniel Fisher, "How Sir John Browne Turned BP Amoco into the Hottest Prospect in the Oil Patch," *Forbes*, April 2, 2001, p. 110.

7. Janet Guyon and John Browne (interviewed), "A Big-Oil Man Gets Religion," *Fortune,* March 6, 2000.

8. Ram Charan and Geoffrey Colvin,"The Right Fit," *Fortune*, April 17, 2000, p. 226.

9. Leslie Gaines-Ross and Chris Komisarjevsky, "The Brand-Name CEO," *Across the Board*, June 1999, pp. 26–29.

10. Andrew Davidson, "The Andrew Davidson Interview: John Browne," *Management Today*, December 1999.

11. Ram Charan and Geoffrey Colvin,"Why CEOs Fail," *Fortune*, June 21, 1999, Vol 139, No. 12, p. 68–78

12. James C. Collins and Jerry I. Porras, *Built to Last*, New York, HarperBusiness, Oct. 26, 1994, p. 178.

13. Anthony Bianco and Pamela L. Moore, "Downfall: The Inside Story of the Management Fiasco at Xerox," *BusinessWeek*, March 5, 2001, p. 84.

14. See, for example, Geoffrey Colvin, "Changing of the Guard," *Fortune*, January 8, 2001, p. 84.

15. Robert Slater, *The New GE,* Irwin, 1993, p. 268.

16. "Nine Steps Toward Creating a Great Workplace—Right Here, Right Now," *Harvard Management Update*, March 1999. The Gallup study was reported and analyzed in Marcus Buckingham and Curt Coffman, *First, Break All the Rules: What the World's Great Managers Do Differently*, New York, Simon & Schuster, 1999.

CHAPTER 6

1. Vijay Govindarajan and Anil K. Gupta, "Taking Wal-Mart Global," *Strategy & Business*, Fourth Quarter, Issue 17, p. 14–25. 1999—abstracted from a 1996 case study of Wal-Mart by Rob Lynch, Tuck School of Business Administration.

2. Ibid.

3. Ibid.

4. "Cisco iQ—Wal-Mart Links to Suppliers, Employees," 2000. http://business.cisco.com/app/tree.taf?assetid=49777&level=two& sectionid=44755

5. "NCR Case Study: Wal-Mart's Checkout Gets Boost with New NCR 7875 Bi-Optic AR Scanner," 2001. www.ncr.com/repository/case_ studies/store_autonation/sa_walmart7875scanner.htm

6. Gregory G. Dess and Joseph C. Picken, "Creating Competitive Disadvantage: Learning from Food Lion's Freefall," *Academy of Management Executive*, August 1999, Vol 13, No. 3, p. 97–111.

7. John Huey, Geoffrey Colvin, Herb Kelleher, and Jack Welch, "The Jack and Herb Show," *Fortune*, January 11, 1999, p. 163.

8. Erich Luening, "Home Depot Lays Its E-Commerce Foundation," *CNET News.com*, August 30, 2000.

9. Cheryl Rosen, "Home Depot Revamps Customer Service Strategy," *InformationWeek*, June 26, 2001, http://www.informationweek.com/ story/IWK20010626500

10. Karen Jacobs, "Home Depot Keen to Reduce Store Clutter," *Reuters*, July 30, 2001.

11. Rob Landley, "A Case for Home Depot," *The Motley Fool*, January 14, 2000. http://www.fool.com/portfolios/rulemaker/2000/rulemaker 000114.htm

12. Ibid.

13. George Anders, "John Chambers, After the Deluge," *Fast Company*, July 2001, p. 100.
14. "Merger Integration: Delivering on the Promise," Research Summary, Viewpoint Report, p. 2, Booz-Allen & Hamilton, July 2001.
15. Janet Whitman, "'Strategic' Deals Regularly Fall Short of Goals," *Wall Street Journal*, August 7, 2001.

CHAPTER 7

1. "Wall Street's Spin Game," *BusinessWeek*, October 5, 1998.
2. Peter Elkind, "Where Mary Meeker Went Wrong," *Fortune*, May 14, 2001, p. 68.
3. Emily Thornton, "Wall Street's Chinese Walls Aren't Strong Enough," *BusinessWeek*, August 27, 2001, p. 56.
4. Jeff D. Opdyke, "Many Analysts Found to Invest in Companies They Covered," *Wall Street Journal*, August 1, 2001, C1.
5. Brian O'Keefe, "Rebuilding the Rock," *Fortune*, June 11, 2001.
6. Andy Kessler, "Manager's Journal: We're All Analysts Now," *Wall Street Journal*, July 30, 2001, A18.
7. Amy Hutton, "Four Rules for Taking Your Message to Wall Street," *Harvard Business Review*, May 2001, p. 125.
8. Ibid.
9. Speech by Graham Phillips, "How Communications Becomes Capital," *Measuring The Future*, conference hosted by the Cap Gemini Ernst & Young Center for Business Innovation, 1999.
10. Shanthhi Kalathil, "Asia Gets a Hard Lesson in Cost of Firms' Murky Bookkeeping," *Wall Street Journal*, December 15, 1997, A19.
11. Justin Fox, "A Startling Notion—The Whole Truth," *Fortune*, November 24, 1997, p. 303.
12. Joseph Weber, "Disclosure or Data Glut?" *BusinessWeek*, August 13, 2001, p. 32.
13. "The Cemex Way," *The Economist*, June 16, 2001, Vol 359, Issue 8226, p. 75–76.

CHAPTER 8

1. Kerry Capell with Stanley Reed and Heidi Dawley. "He's No Techie, But He Loves the Web," *BusinessWeek* Web site, January 31, 2000, p. 22.

2. Kerry Capell, "Virgin Takes E-Wing," *BusinessWeek*, January 22, 2001, p. 30.

3. Glenn Rifkin, "How Richard Branson Works Magic," *Strategy and Business Magazine*, Fourth Quarter 1998, Issue 13, Case Study, p. 1–9

4. Becky Gaylord, "Virgin Is in for a Bumpy Ride," *BusinessWeek*, October 23, 2000, p. 37.

5. Glenn Rifkin, "How Richard Branson Works Magic," *Strategy and Business Magazine*, Fourth Quarter 1998, Issue 13, Case Study, p. 1–9

6. Jean Halliday and Alice Z. Cuneo, "Lexus Eyes Brand I.D. Consultant," *Advertising Age*, July 9, 2001, cover story.

7. *Report of the Brookings Task Force on Understanding Intangible Sources of Value: Strategic and Organizational Issues Subgroup Final Report*, October 2000, p. 21.

8. Gerry Khermouch, Stanley Holmes, and Moon Ihlwan, "The Best Global Brands," *BusinessWeek*, August 6, 2001, p. 50.

9. Ibid.

10. "UK dotcoms wasting millions on mainstream ads," *Economic Times*, November 16, 2000.

11. Quoted in Kirsten D. Sandberg, "Building Brand: A Road Map," *Harvard Management Update*, July 2001, p. 9.

12. Eric Moskowitz, "Still Delivering," *The Red Herring*, March 20, 2001, p. 44.

13. Glenn Rifkin, "How Richard Branson Works Magic," *Strategy and Business Magazine,* Fourth Quarter 1998, Issue 13, Case Study, p. 1–9

14. Gerry Khermouch, Stanley Holmes, and Moon Ihlwan, "The Best Global Brands," *BusinessWeek*, August 6, 2001, p. 50.

15. "The Evolution of Cause Branding," *Cone/Roper Cause-Related Trends Report,* Cone, Inc.: March 16, 1999.

16. Glenn Rifkin, "How Richard Branson Works Magic," *Strategy and Business Magazine*, Fourth Quarter 1998, Issue 13, Case Study, p. 1–9

17. Mark Rechtin, "Lexus Plans a Go-Slow Strategy," *Orlando Sentinel*, June 21, 2001, F3.

CHAPTER 9

1. Quoted in Christy Eidson and Melissa Master, "Top Ten . . . Most Admired. . . Most Respected: Who Makes the Call?" *Across the Board*,

March 2000. This article summarizes some of the key methodological differences.

2. Millenium Poll on Corporate Social Responsibility. Environics International, The Prince of Wales Business Leaders' Forum and Conference Board, September 30, 1999. New York Release.

3. Ronald Alsop, "Survey Rates Companies' Reputations, and Many Are Found Wanting," *Wall Street Journal*, February 7, 2001.

4. Charles Fombrun, cited in "Managing Reputation with Image and Brands," Stephen J. Garone, *The Conference Board Report*, #1212-98, 1998.

5. Peter Haapaniemi, "What's In a Reputation?" *Chief Executive*, March 2000, p. 48–51.

6. Frederic Golden, "Who's Afraid of Frankenfood?" *Time*, November 29, 1999, p.49.

7. http://www.public.iastate.edu/~rjsalvad/reports/s00/GMOhunger/hungergmo.html.

8. "Monsanto Stock Takes a Beating Amid Biotech Worries," *St. Louis Post-Dispatch*, October 3, 1999, C1.

9. Carey Gillam, "Monsanto Moving FrankenFood (GM Food) Forward," *Reuters*, March 31, 2001. www.rumormillnews.net/cgi-bin/config.pl?read=8065

10. Ibid.

11. Peter Haapaniemi, "What's in a Reputation?" *Chief Executive*, March 2000, p. 48–51

12. Jane Simms, "Our Actions Speak Louder Than Words," *Marketing* (London), August 3, 2000, p. 29.

13. Nicholas Stein,"Measuring People Power," *Fortune*, October 2, 2000, p. 182.

14. Ibid.

15. Carolyn Aldred, "Disney Cutting Cell Phone Ties," *Business Insurance*, December 11, 2000, p. 23.

16. John Tagliabue, "In a Global Fight, Sprinkles Are Extra," *New York Times*, August 19, 2001, p. 6, column 1.

17. Stephanie Thompson, "Ben & Jerry's Keeps Its Folksy Focus," *Advertising Age*, February 12, 2001, p. 4.

Chapter 10

1. Taken from Idei's speech at The Industry Strategy Symposium, Japan, February 14, 2001.

2. Michael Lemonick, "Gene Mapper," *Time*, December 17, 2000.

3. Bruce Orwall, "Universal, Toyota Set Global Marketing Alliance," *Wall Street Journal*, July 31, 2001, B12.

4. Barbara McClellan, "Brazilian Revolution," *Ward's Auto World*, September 2000. http://industryclick.com/magazinearticle.asp?magazineid=50&releaseid=2455&magazinearticleid=7691&siteaid=26

5. Cheryl Rosen, "Sharing Risks," *Information Week,* June 4, 2001. Rosen is referring to research conducted by Vantage Partners, a consulting firm in Cambridge, Mass.

6. Jeffrey H. Dyer, Prashant Kale, and Harbir Singh, "How to Make Strategic Alliances Work," *Sloan Management Review*, Summer 2001, Vol 42, No. 4, p. 37–43.

7. Michael E. Porter, "Clusters and the New Economics of Competition," *Harvard Business Review*, November–December 1998. See also Michael E. Porter and Scott Stern, "Innovation: Location Matters," *Sloan Management Review,* Summer 2001.

8. AnnLee Saxenian, *Regional Advantage*, Harvard University Press, 1994.

9. Yuri Kageyama, "Sega Hopes for Turnaround by Making Games for Dreamcast Rivals," *I.T.: News from the World of Information Techology,* February 1, 2001.

10. Jay McIntosh, "Strategic Alliances Can Payoff for Retailers in Economic Downturns," Ernst & Young Thought Center. www.ey.com/global/gcr.nsf/us/strategic_Alliances_-_thought_Center_-_Ernst%26_Young_LLP;ay

11. Cheryl Rosen, "Amazon's Alliances," *Information Week*, June 4, 2001. www.informationweek.com/840/amz_online.htm

12. Hoover.com—Business Network Service.

13. Brian O'Reilly, "There's Still Gold in Them Thar Pills," *Fortune,* July 23, 2001.

14. Ibid.

15. Peter Buxbaum, "Making Alliances Work," *Computerworld*, July 23, 2001, p. 30.

16. Jeffrey H. Dyer, Prashant Kale, and Harbir Singh, "How to Make Strategic Alliances Work," *Sloan Management Review*, Summer 2001, p. 1.

17. William Q. Judge and Joel A. Ryman, "The Shared Leadership Challenge in Strategic Alliances: Lessons from the U.S. Healthcare Industry," *Academy of Management Executive*, May 2001 (with Oxford University Press), May 1, 2001, p. 71–79.

18. Peter Buxbaum, "Making Alliances Work," *Computerworld*, July 23, 2001.

19. Julie Bort, "A Tale of Two Regions," *Network World*, April 26, 1999.

20. William Q. Judge and Joel A. Ryman. "The Shared Leadership Challenge." See p. 13.

21. Frances Cairncross. "Trust Us: Managing Alliances," *The Economist*, August 26, 2000.

22. Charles Kalmbach Jr. and Charles Roussel, "Dispelling the Myths of Alliances, *Outlook*, October 1999, p. 28.

CHAPTER 11

1. "Living with Smart Machines," *The Economist*, May 21, 1988, Vol 307, Issue 7551, p. 79–81.

2. "March of the Iron Man," *The Economist*, May 30, 1987, p. 7.

3. "Back to Earth with a Bump," *The Economist*, May 30, 1987, p. 13.

4. "Morning in Detroit," *The Economist*, April 20, 1996, p. 54.

5. "Online Grocery: How the Internet is Changing the Grocery Industry," Darden Graduate School of Business Administration, University of Virginia, case prepared under the supervision of Paul Farris, Landmark Communications professor of Business Administration.

6. "When GM's Robots Ran Amok," *The Economist*, August 10, 1991.

7. Martha Brannigan, "Cruise Lines Go Online—To Tout Travel Agencies," *Wall Street Journal*, August 23, 2001.

8. Timothy J. Mullaney, "Dashed Hopes for Dot-Coms: September 11 Could Turn Expected Profits Into Losses—Particularly for Travel Outfits," *BusinessWeek*, October 15, 2001.

9. "Delphi Automotive Systems: Humming with State-of-the-Art Machines," *Fortune*, September 3, 2001.

10. Michael Hammer and James Champy, *Reengineering the Corporation*, HarperBusiness, 1993, pp. 36–37.

11. Michael Hammer and James Champy, *Reengineering the Corporation*, HarperBusiness, 1993, p. 53.

12. John Ambrosia, "Labor Helps Bring on the New Technology," *New Steel*, April 1994.

13. "When GM's Robots Ran Amok," *The Economist*, August 10, 1991, p. 64.

14. "Success at a Price: General Motors' Saturn," *The Economist*, June 27, 1992, p. 80.

15. Erik Brynjolfsson, Lorin M. Hitt, and Shinkyu Yang, "Intangible Assets: How the Interaction of Computers and Organizational Structure Affects Stock Market Valuations," *MIT Working Paper*, July 2000, p. 1.

16. "NCR and Canmax Partner to Give 7-Eleven a High-Tech Advantage," *NCR Case Study Store Autonation*, 2001. http://www.ncr.com/repository/case_studies/store_autonation/sa-7eleven.htm

17. "7-Eleven Plans Overhaul of Product Offerings," Associated Press Web site, August 2, 2000.

18. "Research Finds Internet Technology Investments Can Boost Business Financial Performance, Productivity," *The University of Texas at Austin Office of Public Affairs*, September 21, 2000.

CHAPTER 12

1. Betsy Morris and Matthew Boyle, "White-Collar Blues," *Fortune*, July 23, 2001.

2. "The Changing Employment Picture," *Washington Post Online*, updated November 16, 2001.

3. "Employee Retention: What Managers Can Do," *Harvard Management Update*, April 2000.

4. See, for example, David A. Hounshell, *From the American System to Mass Production, 1800–1932*, Johns Hopkins University Press, 1984.

5. Barbara Garson, *All the Livelong Day: The Meaning and Demeaning of Routine Work*, New York: Penguin Books Revised Edition, 1994, p. 161.

6. "A Long March," *The Economist*, July 14, 2001.

7. Pamela Sebastian, "A Special Background Report on Trends in Industry and Finance," *Wall Street Journal*, September 30, 1999.

8. Laurie Bassi and Daniel McMurrer, "Training Investment Can Mean Financial Performance," *Training & Development*, May 1998.

9. Steven Lipin and Nikhil Deogun, "Big Mergers of 90s Prove Disappointing to Shareholders," *Wall Street Journal*, October 30, 2000.

10. Kenneth P. De Meuse, Paul A. Vanderheiden, and Thomas J. Bergmann, "Announced Layoffs: Their Effect on Corporate Financial Performance," *Human Resource Management* 33, no.4, Winter 1994, pp. 509–30.

11. AnnaLee Saxenian, *Silicon Valley's New Immigrant Entrepreneurs,* Public Policy Institute of California, 1999.

12. Ronald Henkoff, "Finding, Training, and Keeping the Best Service Workers," *Fortune,* October 3, 1994.

13. "Cruise the GM Experience," *PR Newswire,* June 26, 2001.

14. Jason Hurwitz, Stephen Lines, Bill Montgomery, and Jeffrey Schmidt, "The Linkage Between Management Practices, Intangibles Performance, and Stock Returns," *Journal of Intellectual Capital,* Vol 3 No. 1, 2002.

15. Bill Birchard, "Intangible Assets Plus Hard Numbers Equals Soft Finance," *Fast Company,* issue 28, October 1999.

16. "A Statistical Profile of Employee Ownership," The National Center for Employee Ownership, April 2001.

17. Lucinda Harper, "A Special News Report on People and Their Jobs in Offices, Fields and Factories," *Wall Street Journal,* January 11, 1994.

18. Sue Shellenbarger, "Family-Friendly Jobs Are the First Step to Efficient Workplace," *Wall Street Journal,* May 15, 1996.

19. "UTC Invests More Than $200 Million to Send Employees to College, Graduate School," *PR Newswire,* April 24, 2001.

20. Jack Ewing, "Sharing the Wealth," *BusinessWeek e.biz,* March 19, 2001.

21. See Laurence Prusak and Don Cohen, "How to Invest in Social Capital," *Harvard Business Review* 79, no. 6, June 2001, p. 86.

22. See Etienne Wenger and William M. Snyder, "Communities of Practice: The Organizational Frontier," *Harvard Business Review* 78, no. 1, January–February 2000, Vol 78, No 1, pp. 139–45.

23. "Employee Retention: What Managers Can Do," *Harvard Management Update* Web site, April 2000.

24. Jai Ghorpade, "Managing Five Paradoxes of 360-Degree Feedback," *Academy of Management Executives,* February 1, 2000.

CHAPTER 13

1. Justin Fox, "Nokia's Secret Code," *Fortune* Web site, May 1, 2000, p. 160.

2. Robert Levering, "A New Form of Global Competition," *Exame* (Brazil), September 2000.

3. Marc Hequet, "Worker Involvement Lights Up Neon," *Training* 31, no. 6, June 1994, pp. 22–29.

4. John Holusha, "LTV's Weld of Worker and Manager," *New York Times*, August 2, 1994, D1, Column 3.

5. Alex Markels, "Making Sure Work Is Fun," *Wall Street Journal*, July 3, 1995, A1.

6. John Paul MacDuffie, "Human Resource Bundles and Manufacturing Performance: Organizational Logic and Flexible Production Systems in the World Auto Industry," *Industrial and Labor Relations Review* 48, no. 2, 1995, pp. 197–221.

7. Casey Ichniowski, Kathryn Shaw, and Giovanna Prennushi, "The Effect of Human Resource Management Practices on Productivity," *American Economics Review* Working Paper, 1997.

8. Jennifer Reingold, "Can C. K. Prahalad Pass the Test?" *Fast Company*, issue 49, August 2001, p. 108.

9. Julie Creswell, "America's Elite Factories," *Fortune*, September 3, 2001.

10. Art Kleiner, "Jack Stack's Story Is an Open Book," *Strategy and Business*, Issue 24, Third Quarter 2001, The Creative Mind (section), p. 1–10.

11. Carol Hymowitz, "In the Lead: Psychotherapists Enter the Workplace to Aid Dysfunctional Staffs," *Wall Street Journal*, November 27, 2001, B1.

12. "Using Measurement to Boost Your Unit's Performance," *Harvard Management Update*, October 1998.

13. Jennifer Koch Laabs, "Optimas 2001—General Excellence: Thinking Outside the Box at the Container Store," *Workforce*, March 2001; Daniel Roth, "My Job at the Container Store," *Fortune*, January 10, 2000, Vol 141, pp. 74–78.

14. U.S. Department of Labor, "Road to High Performance Workplaces," *Guide to Better Jobs and Better Business Results*, 1994.

CHAPTER 14

1. Thomas W. Malone, "Is Empowerment a Fad? Control, Decision Making, and IT," *Sloan Management Review*, Winter 1997, Vol 38, No. 2, p. 23–35.

2. Karl Sabbagh, *Twenty-First Century Jet: The Making and Marketing of the Boeing 777*, Charles Scribner & Sons, 1996.

3. J. Lynn Lunsford, "With Airbus on Its Tail, Boeing Is Rethinking How It Builds Planes," *Wall Street Journal*, September 5, 2001, A1.

4. Ibid.

5. Kerry A. Dolan and Robyn Meredith, "Ghost Cars, Ghost Brands," *Forbes*, April 30, 2001.

6. Eric Chabrow, "Playing for Keeps," *Information Week*, December 11, 2000.

7. David Baker, *Scientific American's Inventions from Outer Space*, Random House, 2000.

8. Bethany McLean, "A Bitter Pill," *Fortune*, August 13, 2001.

9. Michael Arndt, "Eli Lilly: Life after Prozac," *BusinessWeek*, July 23, 2001.

10. Pui-Wing Tam, "How Palm Tumbled from Star of Tech to Target of Microsoft," *Wall Street Journal*, September 7, 2001.

11. See Gary Hamel, "Bringing Silicon Valley Inside," *Harvard Business Review*, September–October 1999; and Giffod Pinchot, *Intrapreneuring: Why You Don't Have to Leave the Corporation to Be an Entrepreneur*, Berrett-Koehler Publishers, 1999.

12. Gary Hamel, "Innovation's New Math," *Fortune*, July 9, 2001.

CHAPTER 15

1. Clark Eustace, "The Intangible Economy—Impact and Policy Issues," European Commission, October 2000.

2. Congressional Record: October 21, 1998 (Senate) [Page S12972-S12973], From the Congressional Record Online via GPO Access [wais.access.gpo.gov] [DOCID:cr21oc98–275].

3. Joyce Slaton, "Innovation of the Year," *Smart Business*, January 2001.

4. Alan Murray, "As Businesses Innovate, Regulators Must Follow Suit," *Wall Street Journal*, August 23, 2001.

5. The Social Investment Forum, *1999 SRI Trends Report*, November 4, 1999.

6. Alan Murray, "As Businesses Innovate, Regulators Must Follow Suit," *Wall Street Journal*, August 23, 2001.

CHAPTER 16

1. "The Logic of Global Business: An Interview with ABB's Percy Barnevik," *Harvard Business Review*, March–April 1991, pp. 91–105.
2. John Helyar and Noshua Watson, "A Wing and a Prayer: Numb from Disaster, American Airlines Just Keeps Coping and Flying," *Fortune*, December 10, 2001.
3. See Devin Leonard, "Mr. Messier Is Ready for His Close-Up," *Fortune*, September 3, 2001.
4. John Carreyrou, "Vivendi Is More Buoyant for Its Water Unit," *Wall Street Journal*, August 1, 2001.
5. Janet Guyon, "Can Messier Make Cash Flow Like Water?" *Fortune*, September 3, 2001.
6. See Andrew Tausz, "Still the One to Beat," *Telephony*, August 13, 2001.
7. "Nokia: A Finnish Fable," *The Economist*, October 14, 2000.
8. Ibid.
9. Ibid.
10. Andrew Tausz, "Still the One to Beat," *Telephony*, August 13, 2001.
11. Ibid.
12. Peter Senge's seminal book is *The Fifth Discipline: The Art and Practice of the Learning Organization,* Doubleday/Currency paperback, 1994. See also "The Leader's New Work: Building Learning Organizations," *Sloan Management Review* 32, no. 1, Fall 1990, pp. 7–23.
13. Rick Maurer, *Building Capacity for Change Sourcebook,* Maurer & Associates, 2000.
14. William E. Fulmer, *Shaping the Adaptive Organization: Landscapes, Learning, and Leadership in Volatile Times,* Amacom, 2000.

CHAPTER 17

1. http://www.citizensbank.ca/insidecitizens/ethical_er.html
2. See Peter J. Howe, "Will the Reflection in This Tiny Array of Mirrors Be Bright Enough to Restore Lucent's Luster?" *Boston Globe*, September 9, 2000, C1.

AFTERWORD

1. Andrew Serwer; Reporter Associate Julia Boorstin, 'This is Going to Leave a Huge Scar on All of Us' Wall streeters are resilient, but overcoming this catastrophe seems almost too hard. *Fortune*, October 1, 2001.

INDEX